LET'S LEARN ABOUT...
THE OCEAN

Teacher's Guide

STEAM

K1

Pearson

Pearson Education do Brasil
KAO Two, KAO Park, Harlow, Essex, CM17 9NA, England
and Associated Companies around the world

© Pearson Education do Brasil 2020

The right of Luciana Pinheiro and Simara H. Dal'Alba to be identified as author of this Work has been asserted by them in accordance with the Copyright, Designs and Patents Act 1988.

All rights reserved; no part of this publication may be reproduced, stored in a retrieval system, or transmitted in any form or by any means, electronic, mechanical, photocopying, recording, or otherwise without the prior written permission of the Publishers

First published 2020

ISBN: 978-1-292-33410-3

Set in Mundo Sans
Printed in China SWTC/01

Acknowledgements
The publishers and author(s) would like to thank the following people and institutions for their feedback and comments during the development of the material: Marcos Mendonça, Leandra Dias, Viviane Kirmeliene, Rhiannon Ball, Mônica Bicalho and GB Editorial. The publishers would also like to thank all the teachers who contributed to the development of *Let's learn about...*:
Adriano de Paula Souza, Aline Ramos Teixeira Santo, Aline Vitor Rodrigues Pina Pereira, Ana Paula Gomez Montero, Anna Flávia Feitosa Passos
Camila Jarola, Celiane Junker Silva, Edegar França Junior, Fabiana Reis Yoshio, Fernanda de Souza Thomaz, Luana da Silva, Michael Iacovino Luidvinavicius, Munique Dias de Melo
Priscila Rossatti Duval Ferreira Neves, Sandra Ferito, and schools that took part in Construindo Juntos.

Author Acknowledgements
Luciana Pinheiro and Simara H. Dal'Alba

Image Credit(s):
Shutterstock.com: Macrovector 54

Illustration Acknowledgements
Illustrated by Filipe Laurentino and MRS Editorial.

Cover illustration © Filipe Laurentino

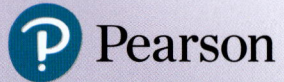

Contents

	Table of contents	4
	Presentation	6
U1	How are we all similar?	8
U2	How are we all different?	16
U3	What is a family?	24
U4	Do you share your toys?	32
U5	How do you help at home?	40
U6	How do you take care of your pet?	48
U7	What is your favorite food?	56
U8	What do you like about school?	64

Table of contents - STEAM

UNIT	LESSON 1	LESSON 2	LESSON 3	LESSON 4
Unit 1 How are we all similar? Page 8	• Identify the color of their eyes and their classmates' • Understand that people can have different eye colors • Make a poster with different eye colors	• See how similar they are through exploring their facial characteristics • Identify, register, and compare their similarities • Begin to understand the concept of *more* and how to compare numbers of things	• Understand that they are part of a bigger community • Identify some basic needs • Think of ways to help someone see well and build something that does it	• Understand what a shadow is and how it is created • Identify the role of light in the making of shadows • Draw a shadow
Unit 2 How are we all different? Page 16	• Learn that being different is natural and everyone is different somehow • Think of ways to compare data about different preferences • Provide a solution to a simple problem using pattern blocks	• Make works of art and notice the differences among them • Analyze and test possible ways to make a play dough doll stand	• Learn to respect different opinions and tastes when decorating a leg cast • Explore basic balance concepts • Develop fine motor skills	• Develop a protection to prevent accidental falls • Group by similarities in color • Reflect on differences and similarities in preferences
Unit 3 What is a family? Page 24	• Understand a story and the sequence of events in it • Organize the sequence of events using arrows • Start to associate colors with preset codes • Group and count elements	• Learn basic concepts of measuring temperature • Understand why the mercury in a thermometer rises and falls • Make porridge and use a thermometer to measure its temperature • Learn about one-to-one correspondence	• Group elements by color and reflect on grouping criteria • Relate colors with codes to follow a path in a treasure map • Make a craft house with shutters that open and close	• Make a collage and practice gluing pictures within lines • Learn that water can remove paint and dirt • Think of ways to build a simple shelter to protect a family from the rain
Unit 4 Do you share your toys? Page 32	• Learn about silhouettes and match two similar objects • Sort objects according to size, shape, and color • Analyze materials and think of ways to build a toy with recyclable materials	• Make up a story about toys trapped in the ice and dramatize it • Talk about ice and how we can make it melt	• Recognize numbers on a die and count the dots • Identify a common symbol of a power button • Learn to press on and off buttons on toys and other devices	• Explore the concept of forces by watching a ball roll • Make a craft slope • Experiment with small objects and see if they roll

UNIT	LESSON 1	LESSON 2	LESSON 3	LESSON 4
Unit 5 How do you help at home? Page 40	• Measure objects using non-standard measuring tool • Understand how big a house needs to be for differently-sized living things • Relate tools and house chores • Make a small broom for the little elf to help at home	• Learn to use hand pointers in interactive games to make a choice • Reflect on what household chores they can and can't do • Understand that paper and food leftovers shouldn't go to the same trash can	• Compare and match items with the same length • Develop spatial awareness • Reflect on possible ways to help the elves clean the top glass windows • Build a small ladder for the elves	• Learn that there are different kinds of houses • Identify shapes in parts of the house • Evaluate different tools to build a teepee
Unit 6 How do you take care of your pet? Page 48	• Learn about sea animals and their habitat • Build the directions for the seahorse to get back to the sea • Compare light and heavy objects • Understand that lighter objects float in water	• Understand what a pet fish needs to live well • Make a craft puffer fish • Use play dough to take the puffer fish to the sea	• Talk about how they take care of pets • Understand that animals sleep in different ways • Build a bed for a pet	• Practice one-to-one correspondence • Group animals according to the way they sleep • Make a sleeping place that fits more than one pet
Unit 7 What is your favorite food? Page 56	• Make slices of pizza • Understand fractions by putting pieces together to form a whole • Practice grouping food items	• Learn about where fruits come from • Understand that some fruits grow on trees, and others in the ground or on bushes • Plan the development of an idea and understand the meaning of *bug*	• Learn to put pieces of a puzzle together • Make an orange tree • Think of ways to improve the tree to hold more oranges	• Learn to put food away in the refrigerator and why this is necessary • Use non-standard measuring tools to check which lid goes on each container • Compare length and identify if it is the same or different
Unit 8 What do you like about school? Page 64	• Develop the sense of touch • Learn about patterns and finding similarities in them • Use pieces of triangles of different colors to make tessellation	• Use mindfulness to relax and learn about their body reactions • Think of a logical sequence of events	• See how colors mix and form new colors • Learn about a new painting technique • Create an artwork of a school using pointillism	• Get introduced to the term *debug* • Learn to identify and fix mistakes and make something work well • Make a playground slide and test it with a ball

Presentation

Let's learn about... is a bilingual program that aims to develop a wide variety of skills and subjects. To this end, several additional components ensure that students work on creative learning, pre-coding skills, STEAM lessons, personal, social, and emotional development and much more. Teachers can find a complete mapping of the components online and suggested weekly planning to help them with their lessons in order to make the most of the cross-curricular proposal. All of the components of the program provide students with the opportunity to build a solid foundation and get ready for the challenges ahead.

As part of the *Let's learn about... Bilingual Program*, the STEAM component aims to encourage students to gather ideas and explore possibilities in order to solve problems and build knowledge from them – and language is the means by which this happens.

The acronym STEAM is used to refer to skills related to five learning subjects: Science, Technology, Engineering, Arts, and Math. STEAM skills are mostly developed through hands-on activities that require students to think critically, investigate, make discoveries by trial and error, and reflect on ways to broaden the possibilities of the application of new knowledge.

Learning principles behind STEAM in *Let's learn about...*

The STEAM component in *Let's learn about... Bilingual Program* was developed based on the following learning principles:
- Children engage in practical problem-solving from a very early age and they are naturally motivated to do so.
- Children's understanding of the world cannot be imposed; the way they relate the experiences they go through to reality will help them develop their own understanding of the world. Nevertheless, they should be guided in order to find answers and discover new things.
- Although applying certain concepts and skills may seem too challenging for most preschoolers, they are generally capable of developing an understanding of early scientific skills; for instance, if they are provided with visual aid, relatable experiences, and hands-on tasks.
- All *STEAM* subjects are somehow already part of a child's daily routine: they may identify amounts and shapes in objects or understand that a ball rolls when they kick it, for example.
- Providing preschoolers with meaningful opportunities to develop creative and collaborative work is closely related to how much they may progress in developmental domains and school readiness.
- Students play a leading role in guiding lessons, selecting and reflecting on possible materials they need for a given project, and reflecting on improvements. Although possible outcomes are provided for all tasks involving creating something new, they should be open-ended and support students so that they can cultivate innovative ideas.
- The fundamentals of a lesson include: asking students questions to have them reflect on a problem, plan and create solutions to it, observe and analyze the outcome of this solution and reflect on possible ways to improve it.

What a STEAM lesson involves

As in any other *Let's learn about...* component, STEAM lessons propose the establishment of a routine when it comes to the beginning and end of a class, such as greeting their teacher, puppet, and classmates, talking about the schedule for the day, and saying goodbye.

The other activities that are part of a lesson aim not only to present a concept to students, but more importantly, they work towards having students perceive an idea through experimenting. All STEAM subjects explicitly covered in a lesson are displayed at its opening page and in each of the proposed activities. Although subjects are presented separately in each of the activities, all these stages integrate in order to provide opportunities for accomplishing the goals of a lesson.

About the subjects in STEAM

- **Science** – Students are encouraged to make use of the scientific method to experiment and make discoveries about the world. This means that science activities require students to think and create hypotheses before carrying out experiments and evaluating their results.
- **Technology** – Rather than using technological devices as the main tool for technology activities, the program provides an understanding of several man-made objects and basic concepts children should learn in order to understand some fundamental principles of technology, such as common terms, processes, and sequences in programming or dealing with digital tools.
- **Engineering** – When students are invited to build something after analyzing a problem, thinking of the needs, planning and designing a possible solution, they are actually going through steps which are very similar to those an engineer goes through in order to develop a product. The *STEAM* component also proposes that students analyze their production and think of ways to improve it.

- **Arts** – STEAM is strongly related to thinking critically and creating. When creating something, artistic skills such as painting, drawing, and assembling something in a creative way are necessary. As well as using art as the means to accomplish a goal, students go beyond and explore ways to solve a problem creatively.
- **Math** – This STEAM subject is so present in a child's life that the simple understanding of the space they have available on their desks or tables to put their school material is in fact a math concept they needed to develop. A few other essential concepts that are learned from a very early age are the understanding of sequences, patterns, problem solving, estimating size and weight, and measuring using non-standard tools.

The purposeful integration of these five learning subjects in the lessons aims to promote a wider range of learning opportunities to preschoolers. ***Let's learn about…*** students should be prepared to combine innovation with taking risks after careful analysis of possible outcomes and engage in experiential learning through problem solving and collaboration.

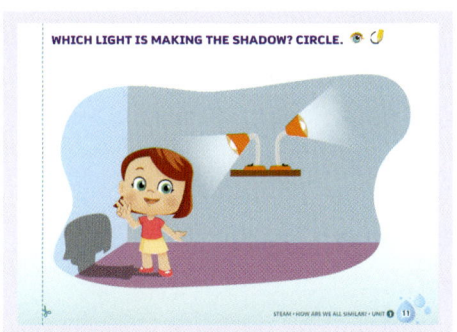
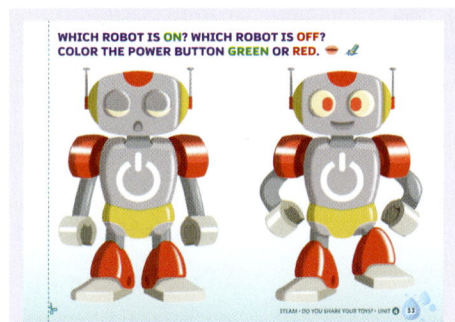

How to work with the STEAM Project Book

All ***Let's learn about…*** Project Books may have their pages removed. Before starting an activity in their Project Books, students can be instructed to take out the page they are going to work on and add it to a folder of their choice, so that students' work can be shared with parents regularly. This page, together with the projects students have developed in other project lessons, can become part of a portfolio created alongside with the teacher.

The aim of a portfolio is to show the cumulative efforts and progress students have made over time. This is also a great way to evaluate their improvement in all learning areas and the mastery of several skills. Students should be encouraged to share the work in their portfolio with their parents so that they can support their child's learning and be an active part of their development as a student.

An assessment chart is available in the Extra Resources folder at Pearson English Portal for teachers to print and fill out with students' performance.

Components

For teachers
- STEAM Teacher's Guide
- Audio library with songs available at Pearson English Portal

For students
- STEAM Project Book with pages that may be removed

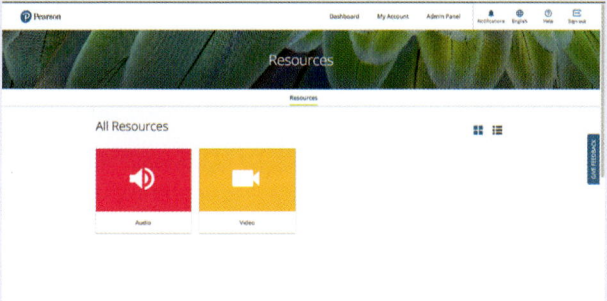

Presentation

Unit 1 How are we all similar?

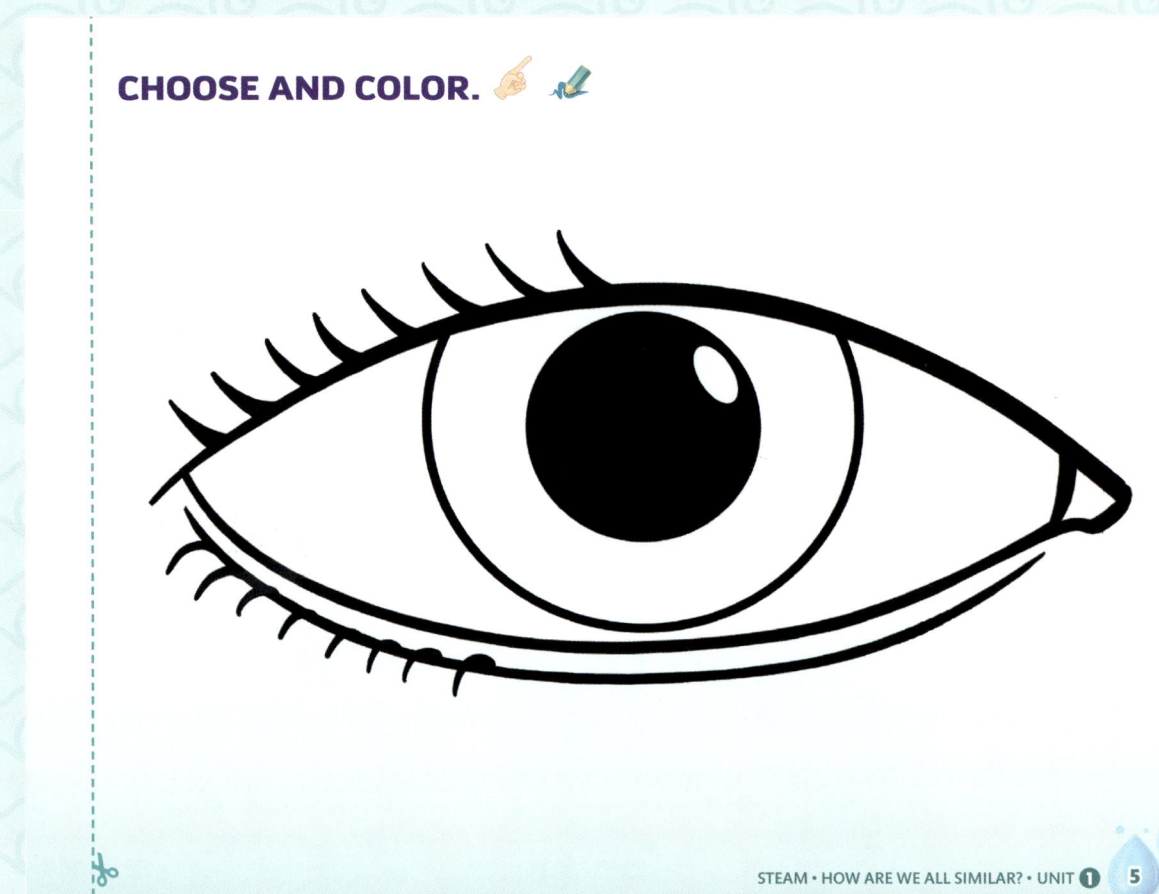

CHOOSE AND COLOR.

STEAM • HOW ARE WE ALL SIMILAR? • UNIT 1 5

Learning goals
- Identify the color of students' eyes and their classmates'
- Understand that people can have different eye colors
- Make a poster with different eye colors

STEAM subjects
- Science
- Arts

Thinking skills
Remembering, understanding, applying, analyzing, creating

Main language content
Who has (green) eyes?
My eyes are (brown).
Are all eyes the same?
The same. Different.
Subjects: *arts, science*
Eye colors: *blue, brown, dark, green*

OPENING

Circle time

Materials and preparation
- Puppet

Say *hello* to students and encourage them to greet you back. Have them sit in a circle, facing you. Introduce the puppet to those who haven't met it or ask for students' help to do so. Teach students the opening attention-getter:
T: *It's time for activities with STEAM!*
S: *And we can't scream!*
Explain to students that whenever you use an attention-getter, they should stop talking and look at you.

> **Note to teachers**
> You can also review attention-getters students have learned so far in other lessons, such as: *All set? You bet!* and *Ready set? You bet!*

What's the schedule for today's lesson?

Materials and preparation
- Visual schedule – pictures of students doing the following activities: a science experiment, a game involving following arrows, building a tower with pattern blocks, using colored pencils, working with numbers. You can take pictures of students with these in advance or print out pictures.

Show students the pictures and explain what they represent. Tell students a few things they can learn in a lesson that works with science, technology, and other subjects. Point to each of the pictures and say the name of the subject, encouraging them to repeat after you.
Then show students the pictures representing *arts* and *science* and teach them these words.

> **Note to teachers**
> Some of the STEAM subjects will still be a little unclear to students, and they are unlikely to pronounce the words correctly in the first lessons. Keep repeating and help them understand the basic concepts of a lesson by trying to compare things with their own reality as much as possible.

ACTIVE LEARNING

Science – My eye color
Materials and preparation
- One or two small mirrors

Still in a circle, tell students they will learn to identify their eye color. Some of them may be aware of their eye color, but others may not.
Give students a small mirror and encourage them to focus on the color of their eyes. Model first and say, *My eyes are (brown)*. Have them pass the mirror around the circle and say the color of their eyes. Then ask, *Who has (green) eyes?* Repeat with all colors. Ask, *Does everyone have the same eye color?* or *Are everyone's eyes the same color? Who in your family has the same eye color as you?* You can compare two students with different eye colors to help them realize that there are different eye colors.

Arts and science – Make a poster.
Materials and preparation
- Crayons
- Flashcards: *black, blue, brown, eyes, green*
- Glue
- Pieces of poster paper (one per group)
- Project Book page 5
- Scissors (teacher's use only)

Divide students into small groups, preferably with three or four students each. Ask them if they remember the eye colors they spoke about in the previous activity. You can use the flashcards to help them remember the colors.
Tell them that they will make a poster to show the students in their school that there are different eye colors. Have each member of a group choose a color. Help as needed. Remind them that colors can't repeat.
Help students open their Project Book to page 5 and color the eye using the color they chose. Monitor the activity and ask students, *Is this your eye color, too? What color are your eyes?* Then help students take out the page and give them a piece of poster paper and glue. Tell them to glue the eye on the poster.

Do a gallery walk.
Materials and preparation
- Masking tape
- Students' posters

Using tape, ask for students' help to display the posters on the wall. Invite them to do a gallery walk. Explain that they can't crowd while walking and they should look at the posters attentively. Meanwhile, ask, *Are all posters the same? Do all posters have blue eyes?*

DIFFERENTIATED INSTRUCTION

BELOW LEVEL
Listen and jump.

Take students outside or make space in the classroom. Ask students if they remember their eye color. Elicit a few answers, especially from those students who found it harder to remember it. Explain that you will say an eye color and if theirs is that color, they should jump. Say eye colors randomly, repeating a few times.

ABOVE LEVEL

Do the same procedures as explained in *Below level*, but then have another round by having a few students call out the eye colors for their classmates to jump.

> **Note to teachers**
> TPR (Total Physical response) activities are a great way of learning while playing.

CLOSING

Play a memory game. Say goodbye.
Materials and preparation
- Puppet
- Sets of pictures with different eye colors

Divide students into small groups and give each group a set of cards. Tell them to place the cards face down. Explain how a memory game works and make sure everyone respects their classmate's turn. Elicit the eye color as they turn over a card. When they finish, wave goodbye to them as you say *bye* and have them say *bye* to you and the puppet.

POINT TO YOUR FACE AND COUNT. GLUE.

STEAM • HOW ARE WE ALL SIMILAR? • UNIT 1   7

Learning goals
- See how similar they are through exploring their facial characteristics
- Identify, register, and compare their similarities
- Begin to understand the concept of *more* and how to compare numbers of things

STEAM subjects
- Science
- Arts
- Math

Thinking skills
Remembering, understanding, applying, analyzing, evaluating, creating

Main language content
How many eyes? How many mouths?
Do you have more eyes or mouths?
What do you see?
Touch your (eyes).
Where is your (mouth)?
Parts of the face: *ears, eyes, mouth, nose*
Numbers: 1-4

OPENING

Circle time

Materials and preparation
- Puppet
- Visual schedule pictures

Greet students individually and have them greet you, too. Then ask everyone to say *hello* to the puppet. Make it answer with a *hi*.
Ask students if they remember the attention-getter they learned in the previous lesson:
T: *It's time for activities with STEAM!*
S: *And we can't scream!*
Remind students that whenever you use an attention-getter, they should stop talking and look at you.
Gather students in a circle. Place the pictures representing today's schedule face down in the circle. Have students take turns turning over the cards as you say what they will have in class today. Help them say the words: *science, arts, math*.

Rote-count to three and clap.

Still in a circle, have students count to three with you several times. Every time they say *three*, they should clap. Model first and have them start counting and clapping with you.

ACTIVE LEARNING

Science and arts – Draw a funny face.
Materials and preparation
- Crayons
- Sheets of paper (one per student)

Divide students into pairs and give them the materials. Have students take turns making a funny face and drawing their classmate's funny face.
Then encourage students to compare their faces and find similarities. You can help them by asking a few questions, *Are they funny? Do they have two eyes? Do they have one mouth?*

> **Note to teachers**
> At this age students are unlikely to draw accurate lines. Nevertheless, praise their work and try to focus on specific characteristics, such as the number of eyes they drew or where on the face their mouth is (lower half).

Math – Point to your face and count. Glue.
Materials and preparation
- A tray with cutouts from magazines: eyes, mouths, noses, ears (two cutouts per student)
- Glue
- Project Book page 7

Place all face cutouts together on the tray. Take one at a time and ask students what they are. Then ask, *How many (noses) do you have?* Encourage students to point to their own noses and say *one*. Then help students open their Project Book to page 7. Point to the eye and ask, *How many eyes do you have? Let's count! One, two!* Encourage students to take two eyes from the tray and glue them next to the eye, one in each box. Repeat with the other parts of the face. Alternatively, you can have students draw the parts of their face instead of gluing cutouts. Teach them the meaning of *more* by gesturing. Then ask, *Do you have more eyes or mouths?*

DIFFERENTIATED INSTRUCTION

BELOW LEVEL
Math – Count the pairs.

Divide students into pairs. Ask them again how many eyes, mouths, noses, and ears they have. Then tell them to stand in front of another pair of students. Have pairs count how many mouths there are in the other pair – counting both faces together. Model first. Point to two students' faces and say, *Anna has one mouth. Julia has one mouth. One, two mouths!* Say the name of different parts of the face and have them count the same way you did. Monitor and help as needed.

ABOVE LEVEL

Repeat the procedures explained in *Below level*, but this time have pairs hold hands and walk around. When you say *Stop!* have them stop in front of another pair of students and answer your question, *How many (eyes) do you see?* Elicit everyone's answers aloud. Have them keep walking and repeat, having students interact with different pairs.

CLOSING

Touch your face as you sing the *Goodbye song*.
Materials and preparation
- Audio library – songs
- Puppet

Have students stand up. Tell them that they will listen to the *Goodbye song* and touch the part of the face you tell them as you pause the song. Play the song (track 05) and pause it after a while. Say, *Touch your nose!* As everyone is touching their nose, ask, *How many noses do you have?* and elicit *one*.
Repeat a few more times with other parts of the face. Then have students wave and say *goodbye* to you and the puppet.

COLOR. MAKE A PAIR OF GLASSES.

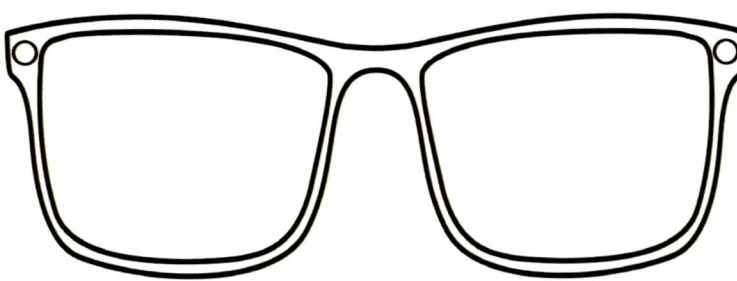

STEAM • HOW ARE WE ALL SIMILAR? • UNIT 1   9

Learning goals
- Understand that they are part of a bigger community
- Identify some basic needs
- Think of ways to help someone see well and build something that does it

STEAM subjects
- Science
- Technology
- Engineering
- Arts

Thinking skills
Remembering, understanding, applying, analyzing, evaluating, creating

Main language content
Are we the same? Are we similar? Are we different? Why can't he see? Can you help?
Colors: *blue, green, orange, pink, purple, red, yellow*

OPENING

Circle time

Materials and preparation
- A bell
- Puppet
- Visual schedule pictures

Say *hello* to students and have them say *hello* to you and the puppet. Make it answer.
Gather students in a circle. Tell them they will learn a new attention-getter. Take the bell and make it chime. Then show students the *arts* picture.
T: *Can you hear the chime?*
S: *It's arts time!*
Hide all the pictures representing today's schedule and have students look for them. Then place them in the circle and have students point to the cards as you say what they will have in class today: *science, engineering, arts,* and *math*.

> **Note to teachers**
> You can use this attention-getter with the other subjects in STEAM as well.

Technology – Strike a pose!

Materials and preparation
- A digital camera (optional)
- A printer

Divide students into groups and have them strike a pose of their choice. Take a picture of them using a digital camera. Encourage them to strike a pose that shows who they are and smile widely for the picture.
Send the pictures to print in simple paper (one copy per student). Place a picture of each group on the wall, one next to the other with little or no space between them, and have students compare the expressions they made: *Sam is happy and smiling.*

12 STEAM

Ask students to look at all groups together. Point to two students in different pictures and ask, *Are they classmates? Are they part of the same class? Is their hair (short)?* Have students identify similarities between classmates and understand that they can work in small groups sometimes, but they are part of a bigger group: their class.

> **Note to teachers**
> If a digital camera isn't available, have groups take turns posing for the picture and drawing their classmates in the other group. Have them also pretend to be taking a picture using a cell phone. Teach them how to pretend to be holding the phone and touching the button on the screen.

ACTIVE LEARNING

Science and engineering – Identify simple needs.

Materials and preparation
- Puppet
- Two different caps or hats

Show students the caps/hats and ask them to point to the one they like best. You will probably have different opinions in class. Ask, *Does everybody like the same things? Does everybody like the (blue cap) more?* Help students understand that people can have different opinions.
Take the puppet in your hands and pretend to have a conversation with it:

P: *I can't see well. (Ms. Gray)? Is that you?* (Help it pretend that it needs glasses.)
T: *What is it, puppet? Can't you see well?*
P: *No, I can't. Can you help me?* (Have the puppet direct the question to the students.)
Ask students what can help the puppet see better. Allow them to brainstorm ideas. If necessary, help them by gesturing with your hands forming circles around your eyes. Teach them the word *glasses*.

Arts – Color. Make a pair of glasses.

Materials and preparation
- Crayons
- Hole punch
- Pieces of string or elastic
- Project Book page 9
- Scissors (teacher's use only)

Tell students that they need to make glasses for the puppet. Ask, *Why does the puppet need glasses?* and help students identify why someone might wear glasses. If they have any classmates who wear glasses (or if you wear glasses yourself), use this moment to talk about similarities and differences. Explain, *We all have two eyes, but sometimes we see in different ways.* First help students open their Project Book to page 9. Have them color the glasses however they like. Meanwhile, walk around and cut out the glasses for them. Use the hole punch to make a hole on both sides of the rim and tie a piece of string or elastic so that students can wear them.
Let students wear their glasses for a while and show them to their classmates.

> **Note to teachers**
> Students at this age are not expected to hold scissors properly and cut paper, so you will need to help them more at this stage. If you prefer, cut the glasses out before the class.

DIFFERENTIATED INSTRUCTION

BELOW LEVEL
Talk about your glasses.

Materials and preparation
- Students' craft glasses

Divide students into small groups and have them compare their glasses. Have them say if the color is the same or different. Then ask students to walk around the classroom looking for someone who has the same color glasses.

ABOVE LEVEL

Repeat the procedures presented in *Below level*, but after students have found others wearing the same color glasses, have them count how many pairs of glasses there are in each color. Help them say, *Seven pairs of (red) glasses. Two pairs of (yellow) glasses.*

CLOSING

How are people in my community the same?

With students divided into groups, ask them, *How are your glasses different?* Elicit the word for the color. Then say, *But for me, you are all similar. Why? How are you similar now?* Help students understand that they are all wearing glasses. Remind them that they are part of a small group now, but they are also part of a bigger group.

Say goodbye.

Have students walk around looking for a classmate whose glasses are different from theirs and say *goodbye* or *bye* to them. Then say *goodbye* to everyone.

WHICH LIGHT IS MAKING THE SHADOW? CIRCLE.

STEAM • HOW ARE WE ALL SIMILAR? • UNIT 1 • 11

Learning goals
- Understand what a shadow is and how it is created
- Identify the role of light in the making of shadows
- Draw a shadow

STEAM subjects
- Science
- Arts

Thinking skills
Remembering, understanding, applying, analyzing, evaluating, creating

Main language content
Are shadows white? Are shadows dark?
What do you need to make a shadow?
Light.
Move your (leg).
Parts of the body: *arm, foot, hand, head, leg*

OPENING

Circle time

Materials and preparation
- A bell
- Puppet
- Visual schedule pictures

Greet students individually and have them greet you, too. Then ask everyone to say *hello* to the puppet. Make it answer, *Hi, everyone!*
Ask students if they remember the attention-getter they learned in the previous lesson. Show the *science* card and make the bell chime.
T: *Can you hear the chime?*
S: *It's science time!*
Remind students that whenever you use an attention-getter, they should stop talking and look at you.
Place both the pictures representing today's schedule face down in the circle. Have students take turns turning over the cards as you say what they will have in class today. Help them say the words: *science* and *arts*.

Play *Solve the puzzle*. What is it?

Materials and preparation
- Pictures of the shadow of a body cut into puzzle pieces (one set per group)

Explain to students that you are going to play a game, a puzzle game. Divide them into small groups. Tell them that each person is going to get a part of the puzzle and they need to work with the members of their group to put the pieces together. Once they have finished, talk to them about the picture they have now. Ask, *Is it pink? Is it blue? Is it black? What is it?* Teach the word *shadow* and have them repeat.

ACTIVE LEARNING

Science – What is a shadow?

Materials and preparation

- Flashlight
- One of the puzzles from the previous activity with its pieces put together

Invite students to sit in a circle and put one of the puzzle pictures in the middle. Elicit the name of the shape you see and ask them if they know how shadows are formed. Ask, *What do we need to make a shadow?*
Use a flashlight to make shadows with your hand on the wall (turn off the classroom lights if necessary). Then repeat the question.
Students will learn that light is necessary and shadows are created when there is an object blocking light.

Science – Which light is making the shadow? Circle.

Materials and preparation

- Crayons
- Flashlight
- Project Book page 11

Help students open their Project Book to page 11 and look at the picture. Ask them to point to the shadow. Then remind them of how a shadow is formed. Use a flashlight if necessary.
Show them both lights on the page and ask, *Which light is making the shadow?* Have students first express their ideas freely and talk to each other. If necessary, position your flashlight the same way as presented in both lights in the picture so that students can compare.

DIFFERENTIATED INSTRUCTION

BELOW LEVEL
Arts - My shadow

Materials and preparation

- Black markers
- Pieces of butcher paper
- Sticky tape
- Source of light (flashlight, a lamp, the sun)

Divide students into pairs and explain that one of them will be standing against a source of light (a lamp, classroom light, sunlight coming from the window) and the other will try to outline their classmate's shadow on a piece of butcher paper. Place the students in the right position and use the sticky tape to fix the butcher paper on the floor. Give out black markers and ask students to first make the outline of their classmate's body on the floor.
If the day is sunny, you can take students outside and do this activity using sunlight.

ABOVE LEVEL

Do the procedures explained in *Below level*, but then ask students to compare their classmate and the shadow. Ask, *Are they the same size? Can you see the color of (his hair) in the shadow?*

CLOSING

Watch your shadows. Say goodbye.

Materials and preparation

- Flashlight

Gather students around their works of art and ask them to observe the result. Ask, *Are they similar? What do they have in common?* (two arms, two legs) *How are we all similar?*
Then have students wave goodbye against the light coming from the flashlight and wave goodbye back to them.

Unit 2 How are we all different?

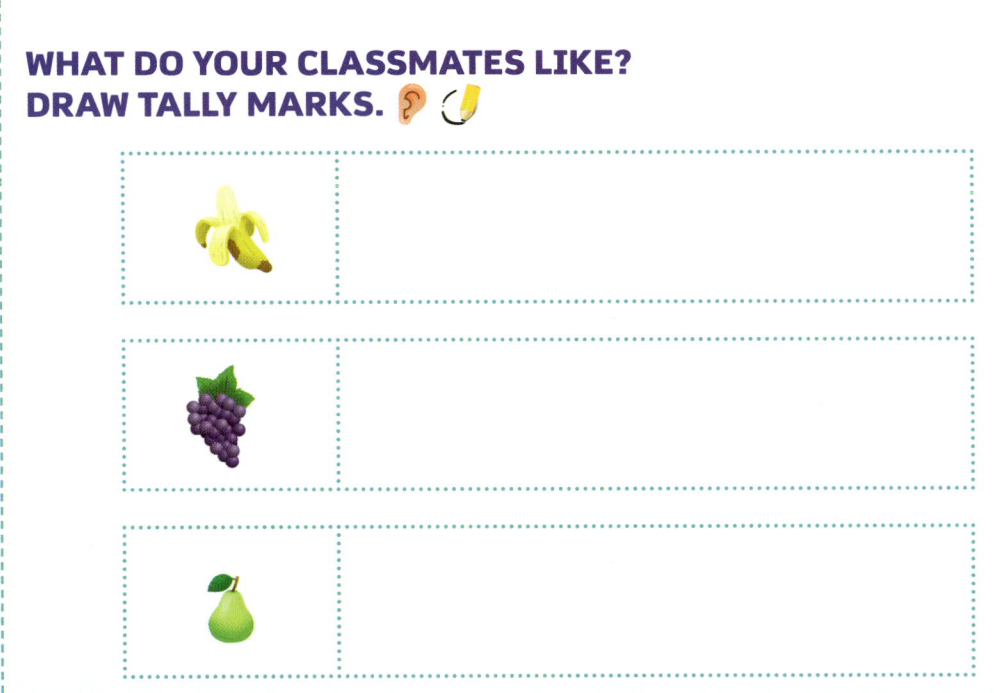

Learning goals
- Learn that being different is natural and everyone is different somehow
- Think of ways to compare data about different preferences
- Provide a solution to a simple problem using pattern blocks

STEAM subjects
- Science
- Engineering
- Math

Thinking skills
Understanding, applying, analyzing, evaluating

Main language content
We are the same. We are different.
I like (grapes). I don't like (bananas).
Fruits: apple, banana, grapes, orange, pear
Numbers: 1-5

OPENING

Circle time

Materials and preparation
- Puppet
- Visual schedule pictures

Say *hello* to students and have them say *hello* to you and the puppet. Make it answer.
Tell students they will learn a new attention-getter:
T: *Can you hear the chime?*
S: *It's math time!*
Hide the pictures representing today's schedule and have students look for them. Then place them in the circle and have students point to the cards as you say what they will have in class today: *science, engineering,* and *math*.

> **Note to teachers**
> Remember that it is possible to use this attention-getter with the other subjects in STEAM.

Math – Grouping according to preferences

Materials and preparation
- Flashcards: *apple, orange*
- Masking tape

Use tape to place the flashcards on the wall. Place them on different walls. Point to the flashcards and ask students, *Do you prefer apples or oranges?* Have students choose the one they like best and walk to that picture. Have students check the number of people in their group and in the other group. Help them count. Then ask, *Which fruit has more people?* Once students have figured it out, say, *(Seven) is more than (five). Our class's favorite fruit is (orange).* If you have the same number of students choosing both fruits, use your own opinion to make the numbers different.

ACTIVE LEARNING

Science – Being different is natural.
Materials and preparation
- Flashcards: *banana, grapes, pear*
- Masking tape

Divide the board into three lines. Use tape to place one flashcard at the beginning of each line. Ask, *Who likes (bananas)?* Use a fruit that not everyone likes and talk about different preferences, *Does everyone like the same things?* You can exemplify by saying, *(Diana) likes grapes, but (Alan) doesn't like grapes.* Allow students to give their opinion about the fact that having different tastes is something natural and say, *Our bodies are different in many ways. We sometimes like different things. We are similar, but we are different, too.*
You can also use this opportunity to remind students of the importance of respecting other people's opinions, even when they are not the same as our own.

Science and math – What do your classmates like? Draw tally marks.
Materials and preparation
- Flashcards: *banana, grapes, pear*
- Masking tape
- Project Book page 13

Use the lines and flashcards from the previous activity to help students do their own survey. Help them open their Project Book to page 13. Tell them that they will choose one of the fruits listed as their favorite. Remind them that they cannot choose more than one. Then have them draw a tally mark on the line next to that fruit. Model first: *I like (pears). I draw a tally mark next to the pear. What about you?* After students have chosen their fruit, have everyone say the fruit they chose and draw a tally mark next to the fruit they mention. Ask, *Which fruit has more tally marks? Let's count.* And help students count with you.

Engineering – How can you show what your classmates like using building blocks?
Materials and preparation
- Building blocks (or popsicle sticks)
- Crayons
- Project Book page 13

Divide students into small groups. Give each group a given number of blocks or popsicle sticks (the same as the number of students in your class). Say, *(Five) people like bananas. How can you show this using the blocks?* Allow students some time to discuss possibilities with their group. Help if needed. Students are expected to take five blocks and place them together as if they were tally marks. Then have students repeat the procedure with the other two fruits.

DIFFERENTIATED INSTRUCTION

BELOW LEVEL
Which one is our favorite?

Materials and preparation
- Colored markers
- Flashcards: *apple, banana, grapes, orange, pear*
- Popsicle sticks (one per student)

Divide students into two groups. Have them pick two flashcards randomly. Ask them to choose the fruit they like best and color the popsicle stick using the color of that fruit, for instance, *yellow* for banana or *green* for pear. Then have students group the popsicle sticks that have the same color and answer, *Which color has more sticks?*

ABOVE LEVEL

Do the procedures explained in *Below level*, but have students pick three flashcards instead of two. After grouping and before saying which color has more sticks, have them count aloud how many of each there are.

CLOSING

Play *Walk, walk, walk… Stop!* Say goodbye.

Materials and preparation
- Popsicle sticks from previous activity
- Puppet

Have students hold their popsicle sticks from the previous activity. Say, *We like different things, and this is natural. But sometimes we like the same things.* Tell them they are going to play a game. Chant *Walk, walk, walk, walk…* then say *Stop!* and have students stop in front of another classmate and compare the color of their sticks. If it is the same, they can say *The same!* and sit together to watch the rest of the game. If not, they will continue walking as you chant again. Go on for two more rounds.
Then tell students that today they can choose a way to say *goodbye* to you and the puppet. Say, *You can say "goodbye" or "bye".* Allow them to choose the way they like best. Reply in the same way.

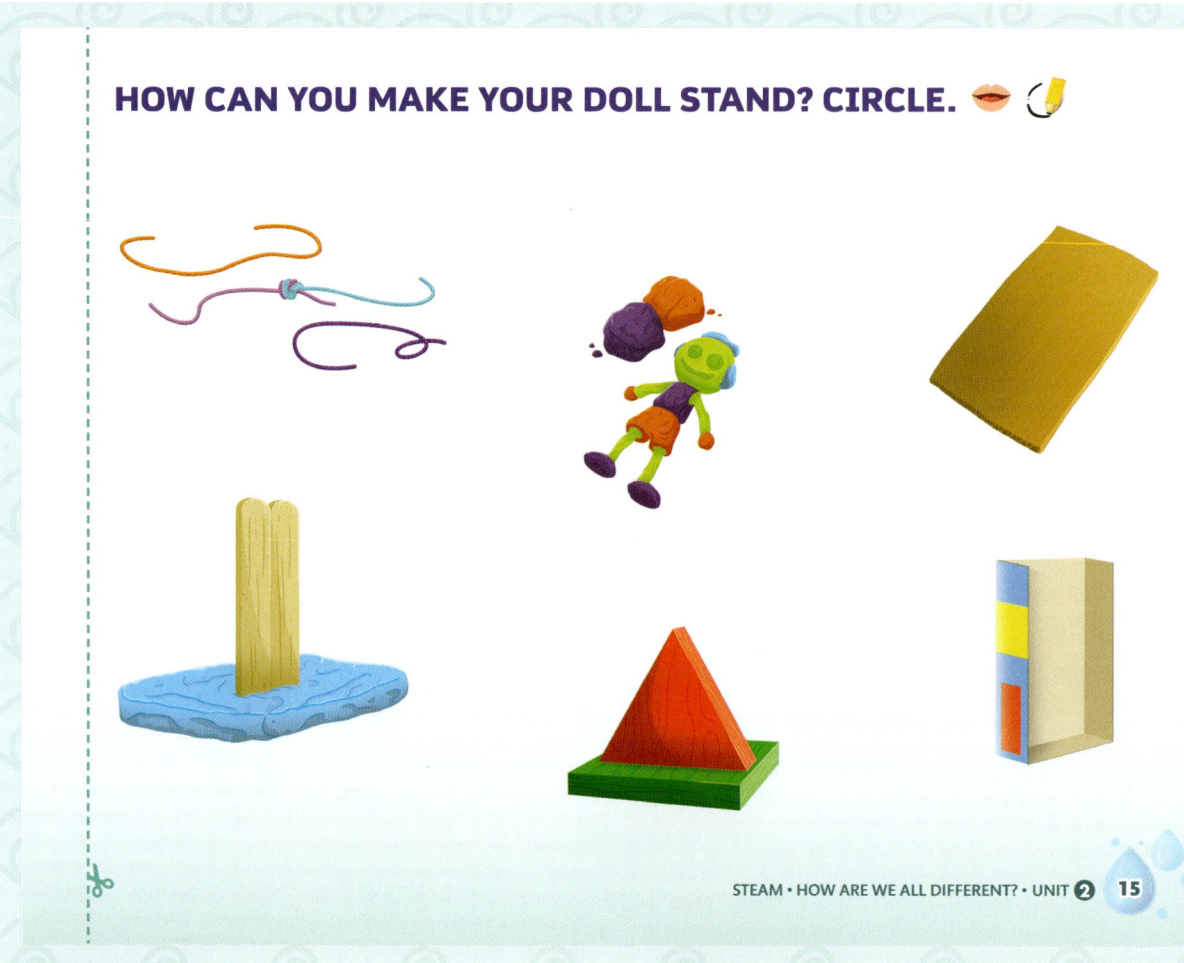

Learning goals
- Make works of art and notice the differences among them
- Analyze and test possible ways to make a play dough doll stand

STEAM subjects
- Engineering
- Arts

Thinking skills
Understanding, applying, analyzing, evaluating, creating

Main language content
Are they (the same)?
How can you make the doll stand?
The same. Different.
Colors: *blue, green, orange, pink, purple, red, yellow*
Adjectives: *big, small*

OPENING

Circle time

Materials and preparation
- A bell
- Puppet
- Visual schedule pictures

Say *hello* to students. Encourage them to say *hello* to you and the puppet. Make it answer, *Hello, my friends*.
Hide the pictures representing today's schedule and have students look for them. Then place them in the circle. Use the attention-getter to introduce today's schedule. Make the bell chime and say, *Can you hear the chime?*
Show a picture of one of today's activities and elicit, *It's (arts) time!* Repeat with the other subject.

Are things around us the same?

Materials and preparation
- Classroom objects

Ask students to get together in pairs and find two things that are different from each other. Once they have found these two things, ask them to come back to the circle and say how they are different. If they use L1, you can repeat after them in English. See if the objects they chose have any similarities. Ask, *Which objects are big? Are they similar? Which objects are small? Which objects are red?*

ACTIVE LEARNING

Arts – My play dough classmate

Materials and preparation

- Play dough (different colors)

Give some play dough to each student and ask them to get together in pairs. Explain that they will make a doll that looks like their classmate.
Encourage students to use several colors for the hair, eyes, and clothes – give them the colors they need – and make the play dough doll show how different their classmate is. You can tell them to highlight a specific characteristic such as the color of the hair or eyes that is unique to this classmate.

> **Note to teachers**
>
> When students are asked to notice a classmate's physical characteristic, they might be unkind. Make sure to emphasize that they should appreciate that everyone is different so as to avoid conflict.

Engineering – How can you make your doll stand? Circle.

Materials and preparation

- Crayons
- Project Book page 15

Tell students they are going to have a challenge. Ask if they can think of a way to make their play dough art stand. Allow them to think of ideas in groups before presenting them with possibilities.

Help them open their Project Book to page 15. Show them the five ideas to make their doll stand. Explain that only one of them works. Ask them to talk to a classmate and circle the one that shows the material that can help the doll stand.

Engineering and arts – Make your doll stand.

Materials and preparation

- A few small pieces of cardboard
- About eight pieces of string (10-15 cm long)
- Medicine boxes with one side and the top removed
- Play dough
- Popsicle sticks

Have students work in pairs according to the possibilities they chose to make their doll stand. Monitor and help as needed. Have them try to explain why they chose a certain material. Ask, *Which one do you want? Why?*
Have students try to make their play dough dolls stand using those materials. Probably only those who chose the popsicle sticks stuck on some play dough should be able to make their dolls stand. If students can't make their dolls stand at first, allow them to try with some other material.

DIFFERENTIATED INSTRUCTION

BELOW LEVEL
Engineering – What else can stand?

Ask everyone to choose some material in the class. Allow students to be creative and take pencils, toys, clothes, erasers, etc. Then have everyone sit in a circle and ask, *Can all the things stand like people and dolls?* After they take a guess, have them check if their object can stand with the longer part placed vertically. Pencils might stand if placed very carefully; a toy car can't stand when placed vertically. Help students reach the conclusion that, just like people, things are different, too.

ABOVE LEVEL

Do the procedures explained in *Below level*, but after that, ask students, *How can you make your object stand?* Have them work in groups and give each group one of the objects that didn't stand. Allow them to think of ways to make it stand, such as by leaning it against a wall, sticking the object into play dough or a container that is just a little bigger, etc.

CLOSING

Do a gallery walk to notice differences. Say goodbye.

Materials and preparation

- Audio library – songs
- Students' projects from this and previous lessons

Place all the projects students made in the last few lessons and have them do a gallery walk. Play a song they like at a low volume. Have them walk around and admire the work of their classmates. Ask, *Are they all the same? Are they different? How are they different? Are all of them (blue)?* Ask questions that help students realize the beauty of having differences in their projects.
When everyone's work has been seen, say *goodbye* to students and encourage them to reply saying *bye* or *goodbye*.

Unit 2 19

DECORATE YOUR CLASSMATE'S LEG CAST.

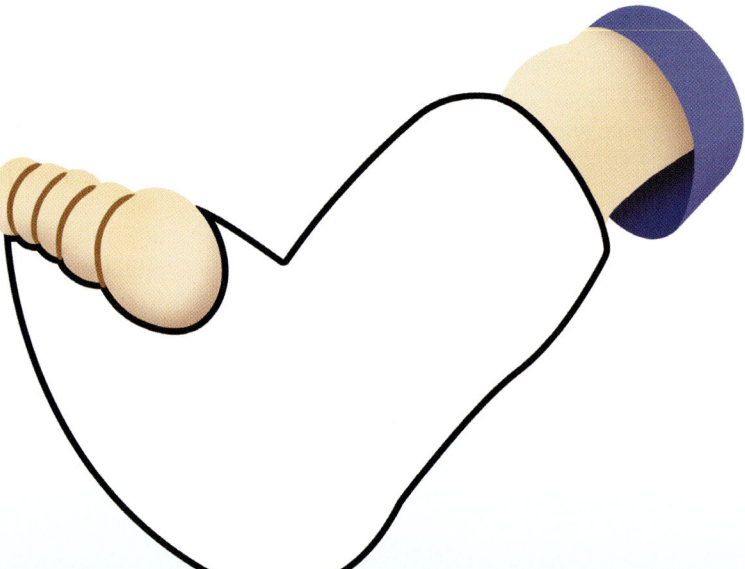

STEAM • HOW ARE WE ALL DIFFERENT? • UNIT 2 — 17

Learning goals
- Learn to respect different opinions and tastes when decorating a leg cast
- Explore basic balance concepts
- Develop fine motor skills

STEAM subjects
- Science
- Technology
- Arts

Thinking skills
Understanding, applying, analyzing, creating

Main language content
She fell off the bar.
It's dangerous. It's safe.
My leg cast is (red and yellow).
My leg cast has (eyes and dogs).
The same. Different.
Parts of the body: *arm, leg*

OPENING

Circle time

Materials and preparation
- A bell
- Puppet
- Visual schedule pictures

Say *hello* to students. Encourage them to say *hello* to you and the puppet. Make it answer, *Hello, my friends*.
Hide the pictures representing today's schedule and have students look for them. Then place them in the circle. Use the attention-getter to introduce today's schedule. Make the bell chime and say, *Can you hear the chime?*
Show a picture of one of today's activities and elicit, *It's (technology) time!* Repeat with the other pictures.

Story time

Materials and preparation
- Big Book Unit 2: *We love gym!*
- Story time accessory

Put on a scarf, a hat, or any other accessory students connect to story time. Remind them that every time you are wearing this accessory it is time to listen to a story. Show them the first page of the story *We love gym!* and ask them if they remember the story. Allow them some time to say what they remember from the story. Then say, *This story is not over. There is an extra part in it*. Turn to the third page of the story and ask what Tina is doing (gymnastics). Say, *Tina tripped and fell off the bar. Poor Tina!* Then ask, *How can we help Tina?* Allow students to think of what to do next. They might talk about taking her to see a doctor, calling her daddy or mommy, calling her teacher, etc. Value everyone's answers and show interest in the students' ideas.

20 STEAM

ACTIVE LEARNING

Arts – Decorate your classmate leg cast

Materials and preparation
- A white sock decorated with drawings that you like
- Crayons
- Project Book page 17
- Puppet

Tell students that Tina went to the doctor's. Say, *Now Tina is back! But her leg is in a cast*. Explain that the leg cast protects Tina's leg until it is fixed.
Put your hand into the sock and show students the pictures you drew. Say, *My arm is not OK. So I need an arm cast. Can you see the (flowers)? I like (flowers)! The puppet decorated it for me*. Use the puppet to confirm it.
Divide students into pairs. Help them open their Project Book to page 17. Explain that they will pretend that it is their classmate's leg in a cast. Say, *Let's decorate the cast. What does your classmate like?* Ask students to ask their classmate, *What do you like?* and draw things their classmate chooses and use colors they like. Remind them that this is for their classmate and they need to respect their likes and dislikes. Model the question and answer with a student. As they finish, if possible, walk around and remove the page so that students can give it to their classmate as a gift.

Science – Exploring basic concepts of balance

Materials and preparation
- A book

Ask students to sit in a circle and retell you what happened with Tina: *She fell off the bar. Now she has a leg cast*. Ask students why they think she fell and have them talk about times when they fell off. Encourage students to use their own words to refer to stumbling or coordination problems. Use a book to teach students about balance. Place it on your palm and use your other hand to press the book as if it were a person jumping on it. First do it in the center. Then go to the edges and press so as to make the book fall. Say, *We need to be careful! Edges can be dangerous. We can fall!*

DIFFERENTIATED INSTRUCTION

BELOW LEVEL
Technology – Don't miss the spots!

Materials and preparation
- Markers
- Popsicle sticks (one per student)
- Two popsicle sticks: one with four dots in a straight line centralized on the stick and another with four dots close to the edges

Tell students that they will help Tina mark the places on the bar where she can step. Show them the popsicle sticks with dots. Have them count the dots. Ask, *Which bar is safe? Which bar is dangerous?* After their guesses, use your index and middle fingers to pretend to walk on the bar. Pretend to be falling off the one where the dots aren't lined up. Tell students that they will draw four dots so as to mark the spots where Tina can step. Remind them not to draw the dots close to the edges. Count with them, *One (pause), two (pause), three (pause), four (pause)! Four spots to step on*. Have them exchange bars with a classmate and use their fingers to pretend to walk on the bar. Remind them to only touch the dots and avoid touching the area without dots.

ABOVE LEVEL

Do the procedures explained in *Below level*, but encourage students to use one hand and only their pointer and middle fingers to walk on the bar.

Note to teachers
Learning about directions and accuracy is very important for preschoolers to understand basic commands they need to operate touch-screen devices.

CLOSING

Talk about your favorite activity. Say goodbye.

Materials and preparation
- Puppet
- Visual schedule pictures

Talk to students about the three main activities they had today and place the pictures in different corners of the classroom. Have them choose the one they liked most and go to that activity. If they have chosen different activities, ask, *Is everyone's favorite the science activity? How are (Sarah's) and (Leonardo's) likes different?* Ask students to help you collect the pictures, tidy the classroom, and say *goodbye* to you and the puppet. Say *goodbye* to them, too.

HOW CAN YOU MAKE THE BAR SAFE?
GLUE THE STRING TO MAKE A FENCE.

STEAM • HOW ARE WE ALL DIFFERENT? • UNIT 2 19

Learning goals
- Develop a protection to prevent accidental falls
- Group by similarities in color
- Reflect on differences and similarities in preferences

STEAM subjects
- Engineering
- Math

Thinking skills
Understanding, applying, analyzing, creating

Main language content
My fence is (blue).
I like (red).
What color is your fence?
Numbers: *1-4*
Colors: *blue, green, orange, red, yellow*
Adjectives: *dangerous, safe*

OPENING

Circle time

Materials and preparation
- A bell
- Puppet
- Visual schedule pictures

Say *hello* to students. Encourage them to say *hello* to you and the puppet. Make it answer, *Hi, my friends.*
Use the attention-getter to introduce today's schedule. Make the bell chime and say, *Can you hear the chime?*
Show a picture of one of today's activities and elicit, *It's (engineering) time!*
Then show students the other picture and ask what else they will have in today's class.

Is the bar safe?

Materials and preparation
- Big Book Unit 2: *We love gym!*

Show students the third scene of the story *We love gym!* Ask them if they remember what happened to Tina: *She fell off the bar.* Then say that Tina is fine now and she doesn't have a leg cast anymore. She is ready to exercise again.
Ask, *But is the bar safe? How can we make the bar safe?* Allow students to give their opinion on ways by which they can make the bar safer, such as by lowering it or putting a protective net around the sides.

> **Note to teachers**
> If students can't come up with ideas on their own when there is a brainstorming activity, use gestures or materials that can elicit possible ideas. You can also explain an idea and ask them if they think it is possible. Be sure to make it as concrete as possible.

ACTIVE LEARNING

Engineering – How can you make the bar safe? Glue the string to make a fence.

Materials and preparation
- Glue
- Pieces of string (four per student, three different colors)
- Project Book page 19

Tell students that they will help Tina to protect the sides of the bar so that she won't fall anymore.

Help them open their Project Book to page 19. Show them the bar and the stakes on each of its corners. Ask, *How many stakes are there?* and elicit *four*. Have students choose four pieces of string and take their glue. Tell them they will need to help Tina not to fall off the bar anymore. Ask them how they can do that using the string. See if anyone can place the string so as to connect the two stakes on either side of the bar. Have the other classmates watch the one who can do it. If nobody comes up with this idea, help them by demonstrating it yourself.

Have students glue two pieces of string, one lower and one higher, on either side of the bar, connecting the two stakes on the side.

Engineering – Make a fence.

Materials and preparation
- Scissors (teacher's use only)
- String (one per group, different colors)

Take students outside or make space in the classroom. Tell them that they will make a fence themselves now. Divide students into groups of five students. If necessary, you can have six students in a group. Have two students stand about a meter away from each other. Have two other students stand facing the first two. The fifth student uses string to make the human fence. Tell this student to use the string to wrap their classmates on each side of the "fence". They will start by wrapping the first two students together and then the other two together. While they are doing that, ask, *Are all fences the same color? Are the colors different? What color is this group's fence?* Walk, monitor the activity, and cut the pieces of string as needed.

When they finish, have them try to walk between the first two students. Help them realize that the string won't let them walk through the fence and fall on the other side of it.

DIFFERENTIATED INSTRUCTION

BELOW LEVEL
Math – Group by color.

Materials and preparation
- Project Book page 19

Pick three students whose color choice for the fence was different and have them sit in different corners in the classroom. Ask, *What color is your fence?* Then ask individual students the same question and have them go to the student who has chosen the same color. Ask them why they have chosen that color. Then ask, *Does everyone in our class like the same color? How are the colors we like different?*

ABOVE LEVEL

Do the procedures explained in *Below level*, but ask students additional questions like, *How did you choose which group to join?* Elicit, *By color.* Make sure students understand the criteria they used when joining a group. Then ask, *How many people with a (red) fence? Let's count! Are there more (blue) or (green) fences?*

CLOSING

Play *Differences game*. Say goodbye.

Materials and preparation
- Audio library – songs
- Crayons or colored pencils: *blue, green, orange, pink, red, yellow*
- Puppet

Ask students to choose a crayon or colored pencil of their favorite color. Have them walk around the room while you play a song of their preference. When you pause the song, have them stand in front of another student and see if they have chosen the same color. If they find someone with the same color, they should continue the game walking together. When all students holding the same colored pencil are together, have them compare which group has most students. Wave goodbye to students and elicit *goodbye*. Have the puppet say *goodbye* to students, too.

Unit 3 What is a family?

STICK THE ARROWS AND CROSSES TO ORDER THE STORY.

STEAM • WHAT IS A FAMILY? • UNIT 3 21

Learning goals
- Understand a story and the sequence of events in it
- Organize the sequence of events using arrows
- Start to associate colors with preset codes
- Group and count elements

STEAM subjects
- Technology
- Math

Thinking skills
Conceptualizing, analyzing, applying, evaluating

Main language content
This chair is (too small)!
Three chairs. Three beds. Three bears. One girl.
What happens next?
Adjectives: *big, hot, small*
Colors: *green, red, yellow*
Numbers: *1-3*

OPENING

Circle time

Materials and preparation
- A bell
- Puppet
- Visual schedule pictures

Bring out the puppet and start by having it greet the students. After they greet the puppet, have the puppet greet you, too. Then elicit *hello* and ask students how they are today.
Hide the pictures representing today's schedule and have students look for them. Then place them in the circle. Use the attention-getter to introduce today's schedule. Make the bell chime and ask, *Can you hear the chime?* Ask students if they remember how to reply and help as needed.
Show a picture of one of today's activities and elicit, *It's (technology) time!* Repeat with the other subject.

Story time

Materials and preparation
- Book or video: *Goldilocks and the three bears*
- Story time accessory

Put on a scarf, a hat, or any other accessory students can relate to story time. Remind them that every time you put on that accessory, it is time to listen to a story.
Read the story *Goldilocks and the three bears* to students or play a video with a short version of this story. Allow students to make comments between scenes.
After that, talk about the family of bears. Ask, *How many bears? Who lives with the baby bear?* Elicit, *Mommy bear and Daddy bear.* Finally, ask students if their family is similar to the bears' family, *Are there three people in your family? Who lives with you? Let's count!* Allow all students to talk about the members of their own family and the number of people in it. Try to make comparisons between their family and the bears'.

Note to teachers

Classic stories may have some variations in their plot. Make sure to choose a book or video in which Goldilocks accidentally breaks one of the chairs.

ACTIVE LEARNING

Technology – Stick the arrows and crosses to order the story.

Materials and preparation

- Project Book page 21
- Unit 3 stickers

Help students open their Project Book to page 21. Ask them what story they can see (*Goldilocks and the three bears*). Explain that there are some extra scenes there. Tell students that their objective is to put the story in order. Have them go to the page with stickers. Ask, *Where does the story start?* Make sure students point to the first picture on the left.

Then use your own book to show them that there are two possible continuations to the story and point to the two pictures that follow. Ask, *What happens next?* Help students tell a little of the next scene and identify the girl peeking into the house. Have them take a green arrow and connect the first and second scenes of the story with it. Then tell them to take a red cross and place it over the picture that doesn't show the continuation of the story. Continue the activity with the other scenes, having students use green arrows to sequence the scenes and red crosses over the scenes that aren't part of the sequence.

Note to teachers

Sequencing and associating colors to codes are essential skills to develop an understanding of how a system works and how to control and manipulate technology.

Math – Group and count.

Materials and preparation

- Pictures or props of three bears, three beds, three bowls, and one girl with blond, curly hair

Divide students into four groups. Place all the pictures/props on the floor. Assign one of the elements to each group: *bears, beds, bowls, girl*. Call one of the groups and say, *Take all the (bears)*. Repeat with the other pictures. Ask each group to show their pictures to the rest of the class and say how many pictures they found: *three bowls! One girl!*

DIFFERENTIATED INSTRUCTION

BELOW LEVEL
How does the story end?

Materials and preparation

- Project Book page 21

Show students your own book. Point to the last scene, in which the bears watch Goldilocks sleep, and ask, *Does the story finish here? What happens next?* And have students talk about the continuation of the story.

ABOVE LEVEL

After doing the procedures explained in *Below level*, ask students to think of another way for the story to end. You can ask questions to help: *Let's imagine the bears don't go to the bedroom and they don't see Goldilocks. What do the bears do?*

CLOSING

Play *Step forward*. Say goodbye.

Materials and preparation

- Copies of the pictures of the story
- Masking tape or chalk
- Puppet

Take students outside or make space in the classroom. Draw five lines on the floor and leave about thirty centimeters between each line. Have students stand before the first line. Explain that you will tell and show them parts of the story. When you show the correct scene, they can step forward and move between the first and second lines. If the picture is not in the correct order, they won't move.

Have the game continue until students have crossed all the lines.

Then say *goodbye* to students and elicit *goodbye*. Have them say *goodbye* to the puppet, too.

LOOK AND SAY. HOW MANY OF EACH DO YOU NEED FOR THE FAMILY? CIRCLE.

STEAM • WHAT IS A FAMILY? • UNIT 3 • 23

Learning goals
- Learn basic concepts of measuring temperature
- Understand why the colored bar in a analogical thermometer rises and falls
- Make porridge and use a thermometer to measure its temperature
- Learn about one-to-one correspondence

STEAM subjects
- Science
- Math

Thinking skills
Remembering, understanding, applying, analyzing, evaluating, creating

Main language content
This porridge is too hot. This porridge is (cold).
Three chairs.
Kitchen objects: *bowl, chair, spoon*
Family: *baby, daddy, mommy*
Adjectives and intensifiers: *cold, hot, very hot, too hot*
Numbers: *1-6*

OPENING

Circle time

Materials and preparation
- A bell
- Puppet
- Visual schedule pictures

Say *hello* to students. Encourage them to say *hello* to you and the puppet. Make it answer, *Hello, my friends*.
Then place the visual schedule pictures face down in the circle. Call on a student to turn over a picture and show it to the rest of the class. Elicit the name of the subject. Make the bell chime and ask, *Can you hear the chime?* Elicit, *It's (science) time!* Repeat with the other subject.

Science – Hot and cold porridge

Materials and preparation
- A bowl
- Story: *Goldilocks and the three bears*

Show students the scene of the story *Goldilocks and the three bears* where there are bowls on the table. Remind students of the content of the bowl: *porridge*. Point to the steam coming out of one of the bowls and ask, *Is it cold or hot?* Gesture to show the meaning of these two words.
Show students the bowl and ask, *Is this bowl cold or hot?* Allow everyone to answer. Then pass the bowl around and have students feel it and check if they were right: *It's cold*.

ACTIVE LEARNING

Science – Make porridge.

Materials and preparation
- A pan
- A bowl
- A spoon
- Bananas
- Milk (or water)
- Oatmeal
- Salt
- School facilities for cooking

Take students to the school kitchen or an area with a microwave. If none of the above is possible, bring hot water in a thermos in the classroom. In any case, be careful with heat and explain to students that they cannot touch the food or water because it will be very hot in the beginning.
Show the ingredients and explain that today you are going to make porridge together.
Ask, *What's porridge?* and see if they can remember this word from the story. Porridge is the food that Goldilocks ate at the three bears' house.
Use the kitchen facilities to cook the porridge. Show students the ingredients and assign an ingredient/tool to each student or pairs of students. Tell them to hand you the ingredient/tool as you ask.
1. Place the oats and milk or water in a large pan over medium heat.
Name the ingredients as you use them. Ask, *Look! This is fire. Is it hot or cold? Remember: don't touch the fire or the pan. It's hot and dangerous!*
2. Add a pinch of salt and stir for five to six minutes. Have students chant *Stir, stir, stir!* as you do so. You can have them pretend to be stirring.

Science and math – Measuring temperature with a thermometer

Materials and preparation
- An ecological glass thermometer
- Bowls
- Spoons

When the porridge is ready, put some in a bowl and have students stand around it. Have them watch the steam and ask, *Is it hot?* Tell students that there is something people use to see if things are cold, hot, very cold, or very hot. Show them the thermometer and explain that you will wash it and put it inside of the porridge to check if it is cold or hot. Say, *When it is hot, this line goes up a little. When it is very hot, this line goes up very much.*
Have students watch the mercury go up and say if they think the porridge is hot or very hot.
Add some sliced up bananas and serve it to students.

> **Note to teachers**
> Always remember to ask parents about any allergies your students may have before serving them any kind of food. It is also important to make sure not to serve the porridge too hot. Wait for it to cool off a little.

DIFFERENTIATED INSTRUCTION

BELOW LEVEL
Math – Look and say. How many of each do you need for the family? Circle.

Materials and preparation
- Crayons
- Project Book page 23

Ask students if they remember how many bears there are in the family and elicit the number *three*.
Help students open their Project Book to page 23. Say, *The bears are hungry. They want porridge. Let's give one bowl to Daddy, one to Mommy, and one to baby bear. How many bowls do we need?* Use your fingers to show students how many bowls they need: three. Then tell them to circle three bowls to give to the family. Count as they circle. Repeat with the other items, having students circle three of each.

ABOVE LEVEL

Do the procedures presented in *Below level*, but have students count how many there are of each item and how many they need for the family of bears. After they have circled the items, have them count how many were left: *Five spoons! We need three spoons. We don't need two spoons.*

CLOSING

Play *Cold and hot*. Say goodbye.

Materials and preparation
- Chalk or masking tape
- Flashcards: *cold, hot*

Use tape or chalk to draw a long line on the floor. Stand at one end of the line holding each flashcard on one hand and have students stand on one side of the line. Tell them to jump to the cold or hot side as they hear words for food they eat cold or hot. Say, for instance, *ice cream, porridge, orange, soup*.
Then say *goodbye* to students and elicit *goodbye*.

Unit 3 | 27

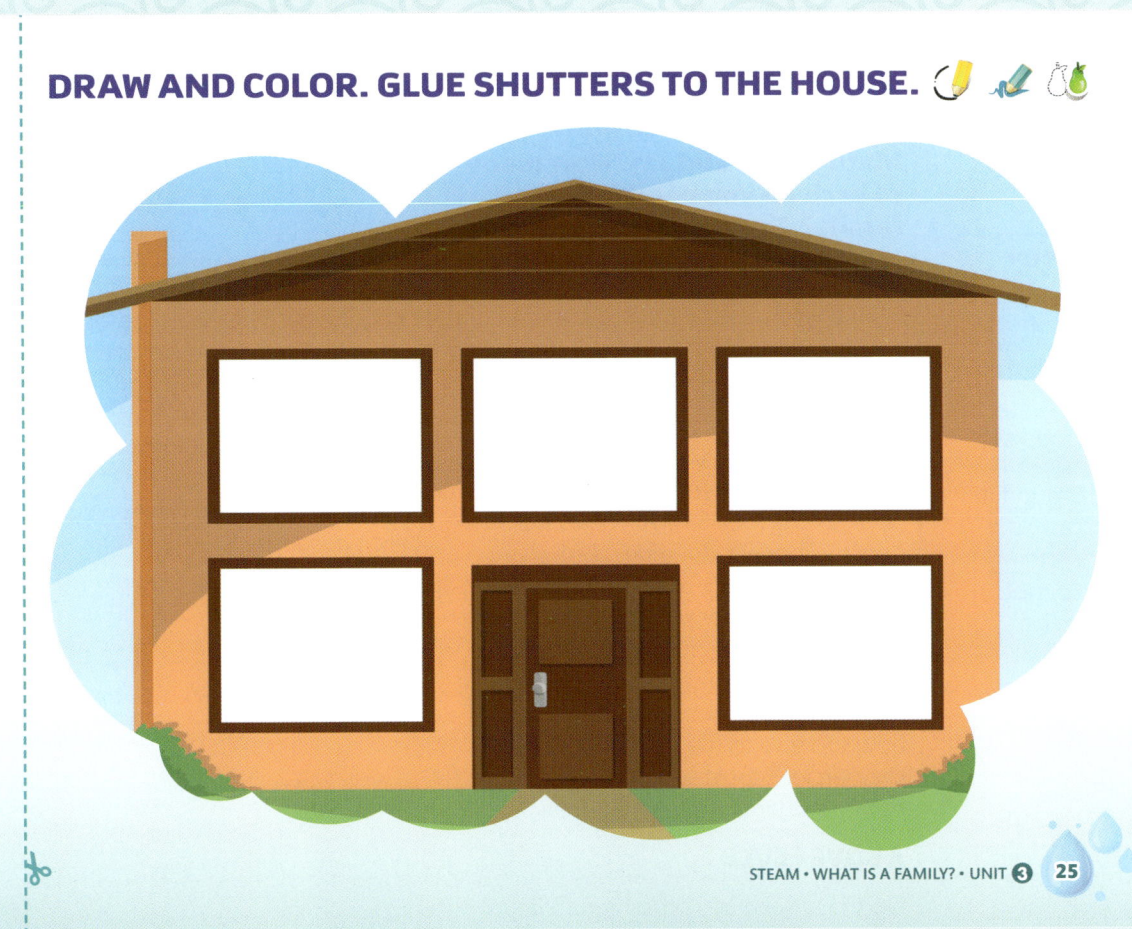

DRAW AND COLOR. GLUE SHUTTERS TO THE HOUSE.

STEAM • WHAT IS A FAMILY? • UNIT 3 • 25

Learning goals
- Group elements by color and reflect on grouping criteria
- Relate colors with codes to follow a path in a treasure map
- Make a craft house with shutters that open and close

STEAM subjects
- Technology
- Arts
- Math

Thinking skills
Understanding, applying, analyzing, evaluating, creating

Main language content
Who is this? How many people in your house? Follow the path.
Colors: blue, yellow
Family: brother, daddy, grandma, grandpa, mommy, sister
Numbers: 1-5

OPENING

Circle time

Materials and preparation
- A bell
- Puppet
- Visual schedule pictures

Say *hello* to students. Encourage them to say *hello* to you and the puppet. Make it answer, *Hello, my friends.*
Hide the pictures representing today's schedule and have students look for them. Then place them in the circle. Use the attention-getter to introduce today's schedule. Make the bell chime and say, *Can you hear the chime?*
Show a picture of one of today's activities and elicit, *It's (technology) time!* Repeat with the other subjects.

Math – Grouping by color

Materials and preparation
- Blue and yellow sheets of paper (one of either per student)
- Masking tape

Take students outside or make space in the classroom. Tell students that they are going to help you make a game for them to play. Give students a random sheet of paper and elicit its color. Point to your right and ask all those students who are holding yellow sheets to stand there. Point to your left and have the students holding blue sheets stand there. Call on a student holding a yellow sheet and ask everyone, *Can (Tina) go to the blue group? Why not?* Help students understand that their group separation was done by color (that was the criterion used to divide them).
Explain that they will place their sheet where you tell them to. Make two curved paths, one with yellow sheets and one with blue ones. Tell students where to place them and help with the tape.

ACTIVE LEARNING

Technology – Follow the path to your family.

Materials and preparation

- Flashcards: *brother*, *daddy*, *grandma*, *grandpa*, *mommy*, *sister*
- Sheets of paper taped to the floor from previous activity

Divide students into pairs. Tell them that they will play the game they helped you make. Say, *This is a treasure map. It takes you to your family!* Model with a pair of students: ask one of them to choose a color, blue or yellow, and a family member their classmate has. Give them that flashcard to hold and have them stand at one end of the path on top of that color sheet. Tell their peer to stand at the other end. Explain that they will move towards their classmate who is holding the flashcard, but they can only step on the color sheets their classmate has chosen. Teach the others to say, *Follow the path to your (brother)*. Have the other students check that they only step on the correct colors and always move forward towards their classmate.

Have all pairs of students play the game. If time allows, have them switch roles and play again.

> **Note to teachers**
> This game helps students understand that following commands and moving along a preset path can lead them to accomplish an objective, which is a basic skill for operating programs.

Arts – Draw and color. Glue shutters to the house.

Materials and preparation

- Glue
- Paper rectangles a little bigger than the windows on page 25 (five per student)
- Project Book page 25

Help students open their Project Book to page 25. Ask them to say what they can see, *a house*, and count the windows: *one, two, three, four, five windows*.
Tell students to imagine that the house in the picture is their house. Have them draw their family members in the windows. If they have more than five people in their family, have them draw two people together looking through the window. If they have fewer people, tell them to choose a friend or two to draw there. Allow them some time to color the picture, too.
Hand out five pieces of paper to each student and explain that they will be shutters for their windows. Say, *Let's glue the shutters, but the windows need to open and close. How can we glue the shutters?* First allow students to think of ideas on how to glue and share them with the class. If necessary, show students how to glue just a small part of the rectangle, making sure it covers the people in the window without gluing anything over them.
While students are working, walk around and ask questions such as, *Who is this? How many people in your house?*

DIFFERENTIATED INSTRUCTION

BELOW LEVEL
Guess who it is.

Materials and preparation

- Students' projects from previous activity

Divide students into pairs. Have students take turns in the activity. One student presses a window closed and asks for their classmate to guess who is in it, *Your mommy? Your grandpa?* Have them open the window of their paper house once their classmate gets it right.

ABOVE LEVEL
Think and find.

Materials and preparation

- Students' projects from previous activity

Divide students into pairs. Have students take turns in the activity. One student presses all windows closed and asks, *Where is my (sister)?* The other student needs to make a guess trying to find the sister.

CLOSING

Count the boys and girls in your house. Sing the *Goodbye song*.

Materials and preparation

- A soft ball
- Audio library – songs

Have students sit in a circle. Take the ball and tell students they will count the number of people in their house according to your question. Toss the ball to a student and ask, *How many boys?* Help them count if needed. Then encourage them to toss the ball to another classmate and ask, *How many girls?* Repeat until everyone has had a chance to play. Play the *Goodbye song* (track 05) and wave goodbye to students. Have them say *goodbye* to you.

Unit 3

MAKE A COLLAGE TO COLOR DADDY AND BABY UNICORN.

STEAM • WHAT IS A FAMILY? • UNIT 3 • 27

Learning goals
- Make a collage and practice gluing pictures within an outline
- Learn that water can remove paint and dirt
- Think of ways to build a simple shelter to protect a family from the rain

STEAM subjects
- Science
- Engineering
- Arts

Thinking skills
Conceptualizing, applying, analyzing, evaluating, creating

Main language content
It's a unicorn family. It's a small family.
Animals have families. Families live in a (house).
Family: *baby, brother, daddy, grandma, grandpa, mommy, sister*
Adjectives: *big, small*
Colors: *blue, green, orange, pink, purple, red, yellow*

OPENING

Circle time

Materials and preparation
- A bell
- Puppet
- Visual schedule pictures

Greet students and have them greet you back. Ask, *How are you?* and have students show their thumbs up to respond.
Have them sit in a circle. Place the visual schedule pictures face down in the circle. Have two students turn them over and say what activity they represent. Make the bell chime and say, *Can you hear the chime?*
Show a picture of one of today's activities and elicit, *It's (science) time!* Repeat with the other subject.

Play *Family clap.*

Still in a circle, tell students that you will talk to them about families. If they think that what you are saying is real, they will clap. Say, *Animals have families. Animals have babies. All families are big. All families are small. Some families are big, but some families are small. All families live in a house.*
Tell students about each sentence and help them understand if it is real or not. You might say, *Animals have families, so they have babies, too.*

30 STEAM

ACTIVE LEARNING

Arts – Make a collage to color daddy and baby unicorn.

Materials and preparation
- Colored paper or magazines
- Glue
- Project Book page 27

Help students open their Project Book to page 27. Say, *Some families are big, but some families are small*. Point to the picture and ask, *Is this unicorn family big or small?* Elicit *small* and have students count how many unicorns there are. Say, *This is Daddy Unicorn and this is Baby Unicorn*.
Tell students that this family loves colors, all colors. Say, *But look! There are no colors. How can we help?* Allow students to give some suggestions. If nobody mentions a collage or colored paper, say, *Hey! I know! Let's use colored paper to make the family very beautiful*. Give out the materials and have students tear up small pieces of paper of different colors and glue them onto the unicorns. Help them work within the outlines.

> **Note to teachers**
> Activities with coloring or gluing elements within an outline help students develop their fine motor skills. In addition, it teaches them to mind and respect boundaries. At this age they are not likely to excel at it, but it is not too early to start practicing.

Science – Washing off the paint

Materials and preparation
- Buckets filled with water (if school facilities aren't available)
- Paint (any color)

Have students choose a color from the paints you have available. Tell them to put the tip of their index finger into the paint. Ask, *Is it possible to remove the paint?* Ask students how they think they could remove it. If they mention *water*, say, *Let's wash off the paint*.
Take students to a washroom or bring buckets filled with water. Tell them to put their finger with paint into the water and scrub it. Ask, *What happens?* Help them realize that the paint is going away.

DIFFERENTIATED INSTRUCTION

BELOW LEVEL
Engineering – Help protect the unicorns from the rain.

Materials and preparation
- Glue
- Pieces of string (three per student)
- Project Book page 27

Tell students that it often rains where the unicorn family lives. Say, *Rain is water. Water washes off the paint. Oh, no! The colors on the unicorns! Let's help the unicorn family!*
As a class, ask students how they can protect the unicorns using three pieces of string. Have everyone brainstorm ideas together and help students by placing one of the strings for them, if necessary.

They could make a tent with it, having one piece of string above the unicorns and one on each side.

ABOVE LEVEL

Do the procedures explained in *Below level*, but instead of having the whole group discuss ideas to protect the unicorn family from the rain, have them work in small groups and then present their ideas to the class before applying them.

CLOSING

Talk about your favorite activity. Say goodbye.

Materials and preparation
- Visual schedule pictures

Have students sit in a circle and place all the visual schedule pictures in the middle. Recall the activities they have had in the last three lessons and have them say if they liked the activity or not. Finally, ask each student to say what their favorite activity was and say *goodbye* to them individually.

Unit 4 Do you share your toys?

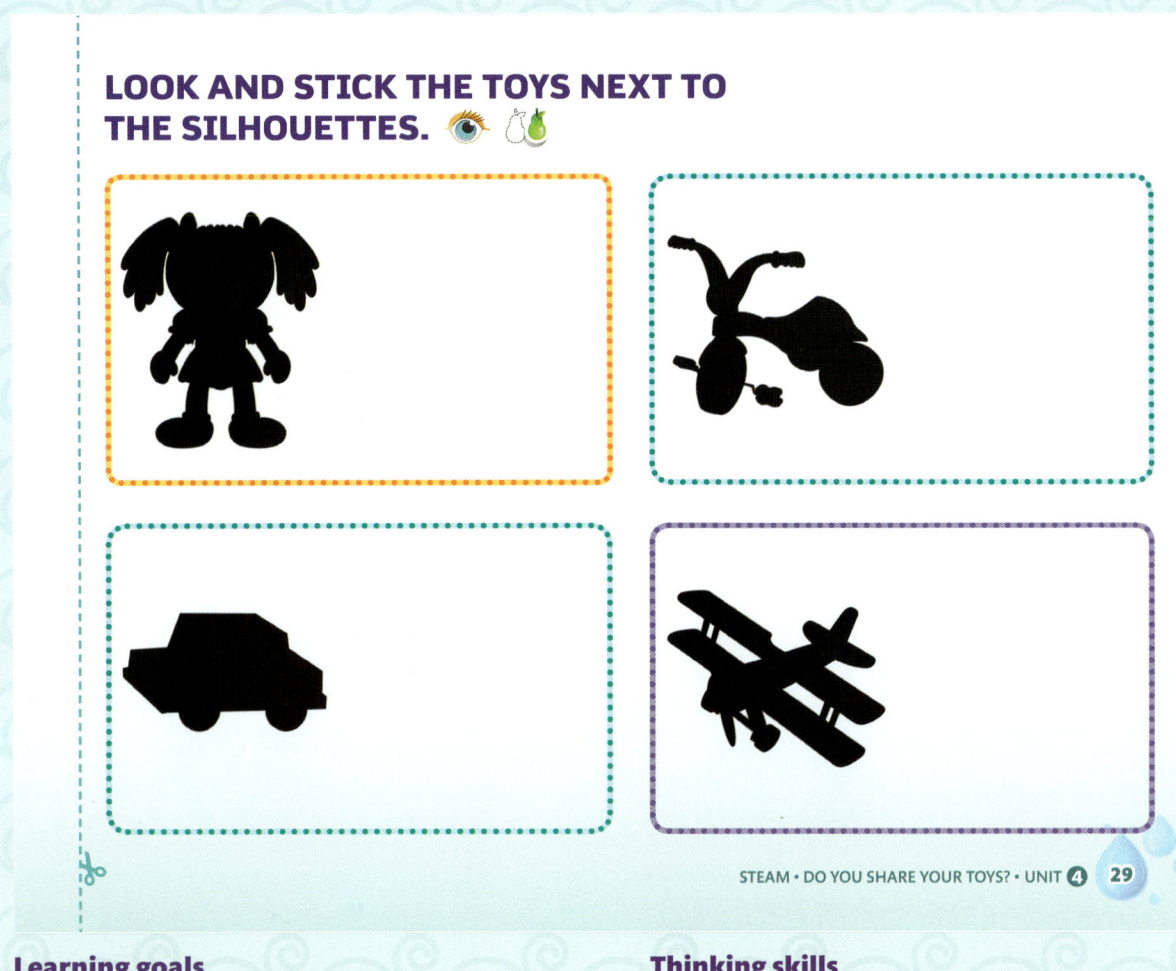

Learning goals
- Learn about silhouettes and match two similar objects
- Sort objects according to size, shape, and color
- Analyze materials and think of ways to build a toy with recyclable materials

STEAM subjects
- Engineering
- Math
- Arts

Thinking skills
Remembering, understanding, applying, analyzing, creating, evaluating

Main language content
What toy is it? Is it small?
The doll is big. The doll is orange and green.
Shapes: *circle, square, triangle*
Colors: *blue, green, orange, pink, red, yellow*
Toys: *ball, doll, plane, tricycle*
Numbers: *1-5*

OPENING

Circle time

Materials and preparation
- A bell
- Puppet
- Visual schedule pictures

Bring out the puppet and start by having it greet the students. After they greet the puppet, have the puppet greet you, too. Then elicit *hello* and ask students how they are today. Show them how to respond using their thumbs.
Hide the pictures representing today's schedule and have students look for them. Ask those who found the pictures to say what they will learn today. Help as needed.
Make the bell chime and ask, *Can you hear the chime?* Show a picture of one of today's activities and elicit, *It's (engineering) time!* Repeat with the other subjects.

Math – Group the shapes.

Materials and preparation
- A beanbag
- A piece of chalk or masking tape
- Small paper squares, triangles, and circles (about twice the number of students)

Take students outside or make space in the classroom. Use chalk or tape to make triangles, squares, and circles on the floor. Have students stand in a line and throw the beanbag toward the shapes. The students who are watching need to name the shape the beanbag falls onto. When they tell you the name, their classmate can take a corresponding paper shape and place it on that shape.
When everyone has had a turn, ask students to check if all shapes are in the correct group.

ACTIVE LEARNING

Math – Look and stick the toys next to the silhouettes.

Materials and preparation
- Project Book page 29
- Stickers

Help students open their Project Book to page 29. Have them guess the toys. Point to the doll and ask, *Are dolls all black like this? Where are the eyes? Where is the mouth?*

Explain to students that these toy-shaped shadows are called silhouettes.

Tell them to go to the stickers page. Ask, *What toy is this? Is it big? Is it small? What color is it?*

Ask students to stick the pictures of toys next to their silhouette. Have them compare their choices with a classmate's before correcting as a class.

> **Note to teachers**
> Matching shapes, shadows, and silhouettes with the objects they correspond to helps students develop logical thinking.

Engineering and arts – Make a toy out of recyclable materials.

Materials and preparation
- An assortment of recyclable and craft materials, such as:
  - Bottle caps (not too small)
  - Colored markers
  - Glue
  - Masking tape
  - Medicine boxes
  - Plastic bottles
  - Popsicle sticks
  - Scissors (teacher's use only)
  - Small plastic containers
  - String
  - TP rolls

Divide students into pairs. Have them think of toys they like and decide on a toy both of them would like to make. Elicit the names of the toys. If students use L1, repeat the name of the toy using English. Distribute the materials and have students think of ways they can use those to build their toy. You can give them a few ideas if you notice that they are struggling to think of ways to build it.

Suggestions:

A toy car – Use four bottle caps and medicine boxes.

A doll – Use a plastic bottle or a TP roll, popsicle sticks (for arms and legs) and string (for the hair).

A plane – Use two and a half popsicle sticks.

A tricycle – Use two and a half popsicle sticks (half for the handles) and three bottle caps.

DIFFERENTIATED INSTRUCTION

BELOW LEVEL
Math: Sort out the toys.

Materials and preparation
- Students' toys from previous activity

Divide the class into two groups. Have each student show their toy, saying what it is and the colors and shapes in it. Then have students sort out their toys according to what they are: all dolls together, all cars together, etc. Tell them to count how many of each there are.

ABOVE LEVEL

Do the procedures explained in *Below level*, but have students think of other ways by which they can sort out their objects, such as the colors in them and the shapes of the toy parts.

CLOSING

Play *The same or different*. Say goodbye.

Materials and preparation
- Students' toys from previous activities

Tell students to hold their toys and walk around the classroom. When you say *stop*, they need to stand in front of another classmate and say if their toy is the same or different. Model first. Have students play a few rounds before ending the class and saying *goodbye* to them.

> **Note to teachers**
> The day before your next class, put a small toy or toys inside the plastic cups and fill the cups with water. Leave them in the freezer overnight.

OPENING

Circle time

Materials and preparation
- A bell
- Puppet
- Visual schedule pictures

Say *hello* to students. Encourage them to say *hello* to you and the puppet. Make it answer, *Hello, my friends.*
Then place the visual schedule pictures face down in the circle. Call on a student to turn over a picture and show it to the rest of the class. Elicit the name of the subject. Make the bell chime and ask, *Can you hear the chime?* Elicit, *It's (science) time!* Repeat with the other subject.

Play *Freeze!*

Materials and preparation
- Audio library – songs

Play a song of students' choice and tell them to dance and sing along. Explain that as you pause the song, you will say *Freeze!* and they will pretend to be frozen, standing still until you play the song again.

Learning goals
- Make up a story about toys trapped in the ice and dramatize it
- Talk about ice and how we can make it melt

STEAM subjects
- Science
- Arts

Thinking skills
Remembering, understanding, applying, analyzing, creating, evaluating

Main language content
What's this?
It's ice. It's water. It's salt.
Toys: *ball, doll, plane, robot, tricycle*
Adjectives: *cold, frozen, hot*
Foods and drinks: *ice, ice cream, salt, soup, water*

ACTIVE LEARNING

Science and arts – How did the toys end up frozen?

Materials and preparation
- Plastic cups
- Plastic plates (one per student)
- Several small toys

Bring the frozen plastic cups you prepared the day before into the classroom and turn them upside down on a plastic plate in front of each student. Explain to students that some toys were frozen by accident last night and today we are going to free them.
First point to the ice around the toy and ask, *What's this?* If they say *ice*, ask students how they think ice is formed. Explain the basic concept behind forming ice by placing water into a freezer.
Divide students into groups and have them make up a story explaining how the toys ended up in the cup of water that was accidentally put in the freezer.
Monitor the activity and help as needed. Then invite students to share their thoughts and dramatize them.
If necessary, brainstorm ideas with your students of what could have happened to the toys. For example, they were on a picnic and ended up in the freezer, they were running away from their owner, etc. Encourage students to use their imagination and make up a crazy story.

> **Note to teachers**
> If your students are curious about the role of a freezer in making ice, tell them a little about the concept of temperature, but do not use numbers yet. Tell them that when the temperature is very cold, water turns into ice, and freezers can keep the temperature that cold.

Science – What can you use to melt ice? Circle.

Materials and preparation
- A piece of aluminum foil
- Blue food coloring
- Project Book page 31
- Rock salt
- Spoons
- Toothpicks

Tell students that they will think of ways to free the toys from their ice prison. Provide students with a spoon, toothpicks, and some salt. Have them think which of these tools is going to be more effective in freeing the poor toys. Use a little blue food coloring for a nicer effect while the ice is melting.
Exchange ideas with students and have them tell you how each of the tools worked. Ask, *Which one melted ice the fastest?* (the salt). Explain that salt helps melt ice and prevents it from re-freezing. Help students open their Project Book to page 31 and circle the tool that could melt ice.

DIFFERENTIATED INSTRUCTION

BELOW LEVEL
What can you find in your refrigerator?

Have students work in groups and think of things they can find in a refrigerator, especially food. If necessary, help them by asking a few questions: *Is there (soap) in your refrigerator? Is there (ice cream) in your refrigerator?* Then have them share their conclusions with the rest of the class.

ABOVE LEVEL

Have students work in small groups and talk about foods they eat that are frozen and that are hot. Have them share their ideas with the rest of the class.

CLOSING

Talk about snow and ice. Say goodbye.

Materials and preparation
- Puppet

Talk to students about snow. Ask, *When we see snow, is it cold or hot? What's snow made of?* Help students understand that both snow and ice form when water freezes. Wave and say *goodbye* to your students and have them wave back to you. Use the puppet to say *goodbye* to them, too.

WHICH ROBOT IS ON? WHICH ROBOT IS OFF? COLOR THE POWER BUTTON GREEN OR RED.

STEAM • DO YOU SHARE YOUR TOYS? • UNIT 4 • 33

Learning goals
- Recognize numbers on a die and count the dots
- Identify a common symbol of a power button
- Learn to press on and off buttons on toys and other devices

STEAM subjects
- Technology
- Math

Thinking skills
Conceptualizing, understanding, applying, analyzing

Main language content
Turn it on. Turn it off.
It's green. It's on. It's red. It's off.
Press the button.
Toys: *ball, car, die, doll, robot*
Numbers: *1-6*
Colors: *green, red*

OPENING

Circle time

Materials and preparation
- A bell
- A book
- Puppet
- Visual schedule pictures

Say *hello* to students. Encourage them to say *hello* to you and the puppet. Make it answer, *Hello, my friends.* Then invite students to sit in a circle.

Cover the pictures of today's schedule using a book. Hold the pictures behind the book and show part of them only. Ask students if they can guess what activity it is. Repeat with the other picture.

Show one picture at a time, make the bell chime, and ask, *Can you hear the chime?*

Elicit, *It's (technology) time!* Repeat with the other subject.

Math – Roll the die.

Materials and preparation
- A die (if possible, a big colorful one)

Still in a circle, have students stand up. Show them the die and ask what it is. Then ask, *What can you see here?* as you point to one side of the die. Help them count the number of dots in the die. Then toss the die to a student and invite them to roll the die. Ask everyone to count the dots. Repeat until everyone has had a chance to roll the die.

36 STEAM

ACTIVE LEARNING

Math – Play *Count and move*.

Materials and preparation
- Masking tape or chalk
- Two dice

Take students outside or make space in the classroom. Draw a start line and a finish line for students to race using the dice. Divide them into pairs and have two pairs at a time play the game. One student in each pair rolls the die and identifies the number on it. Their classmate walks forward the same number of steps as the number in the die. Have them always roll the dice at the same time. The first student to cross the line wins. Then have the next two pairs of students play.

Technology – Which robot is on? Which robot is off? Color the power button green or red.

Materials and preparation
- Any electronic device in which the switch turns green when on (or pictures of a device showing a green on button and a red off button)
- Crayons (green and red)
- Project Book page 33

Show students the electronic device (or pictures) you brought to class. Show the *on* button and ask, *What happens when I press this button?* After students have made their guesses, press (or pretend to press) the button and show them the green light. Say, *It's on! The light is green.* Ask students what happens if you press it again (or press the other button). Say, *It's off. The light is red.*

Ask students what things have buttons and if they can think of a toy they have with an on and off button. Allow everyone to talk about their toys.

Help students open their Project Book to page 33 and have them look at the pictures. Ask, *What toy can you see? How many robots?* Point to the symbol on the robot's chest and say, *This is a very common on and off button. When it is on, what color is it?* If students don't remember the color, use the device or pictures to remind them of that. Ask, *When it is off, what color is it?* Have students take a green and a red crayon and identify the robot which is on and the robot which is off. Tell them to color the buttons green or red.

Have them compare with a classmate and explain why they think the robot is on or off. Help them with the language as needed.

> **Note to teachers**
> As even touchscreen devices have a symbol that represents the power switch, learning about pressing buttons and what the colors of the lights mean is an important skill for using many technological devices.

DIFFERENTIATED INSTRUCTION

BELOW LEVEL
Play *Press the button*.

Materials and preparation
- Masking tape
- Pieces of red and green paper taped on the wall (there must be a red and a green piece next to each other every time)

Have students pretend to be toys. Ask, *What toys have on and off buttons? Do balls have on and off buttons?* Tell students to choose a toy with buttons to play a pretend game. In pairs, have students give each other commands by pretending to be pressing an on and off switch. The switch will be the green and red pieces of paper on the wall. Have them press and say *on* for their classmates to start moving pretending to be that toy. Then have them press and say *off* for their classmate to stop moving.
Make sure all students have a turn pressing buttons and being toys.

ABOVE LEVEL

Have students pretend to be toys. Ask, *What toys have on and off buttons? Do balls have on and off buttons?* Tell students to choose a toy with buttons to play a pretend game. Have them say what toy they are and stand at a corner of the classroom. Have all toys of the same kind stay together. Then tell students to count how many of each there are.

In the same groups, have a student give their classmates commands by pretending to be pressing an on and off switch. The switch will be the green and red pieces of paper on the wall. Have them press and say *on* for their classmates to start moving pretending to be that toy. Then have them press and say *off* for their classmate to stop moving.
Make sure all students in a group have a turn pressing buttons.

CLOSING

Talk about what you liked best in this project. Say goodbye.

Materials and preparation
- Visual schedule pictures

Have students in a circle. Spread the visual schedule pictures in the middle and ask students if they remember what they have learned throughout the last three lessons. Help them remember the activities and ask them all what their favorite activity was. Then say *goodbye* to your students while waving and have them wave goodbye back.

MATCH THE BALL WITH THE SLOPE IT ROLLED DOWN.

STEAM • DO YOU SHARE YOUR TOYS? • UNIT 4 35

Learning goals
- Explore the concept of forces by watching a ball roll
- Make a craft slope
- Experiment with small objects and see if they roll

STEAM subjects
- Science
- Engineering
- Arts
- Math

Thinking skills
Remembering, conceptualizing, applying, analyzing, creating, evaluating

Main language content
It's a slope. Marbles roll down. They don't roll down.
Directions: *down, up*
Toys: *ball, car, doll, marbles*

OPENING

Circle time

Materials and preparation
- A bell
- Puppet
- Visual schedule pictures

Greet students and have them greet you back. Ask, *How are you?* and have students show their thumbs up to respond.
Have them sit in a circle. Place the visual schedule pictures face down in the circle. Have two students turn them over and say what activity they represent. Make the bell chime and say, *Can you hear the chime?*
Show a picture of one of today's activities and elicit, *It's (engineering) time!* Repeat with the other subjects.

Where will the ball go?

Materials and preparation
- A ball
- A piece of flat wood (optional)

Make a slope using a piece of flat wood or place a few books or other thick objects under the legs on one side of a table so as to make it crooked.
Show students the ball and ask what toy it is. Ask about its shape and color, too. Then place the ball in the middle of the slope and ask, *Where will the ball go? Up or down?* Point to the directions as you say the words. Allow all students to make a guess before releasing the ball. Invite a few students to try and see if the ball continues to move downwards.

ACTIVE LEARNING

Science and math – Match the ball with the slope it rolled down.

Materials and preparation
- Crayons
- Project Book page 35

Help students open their Project Book to page 35. Point to the ball and ask, *What is it?* Say that the ball is rolling down one of the ramps. Ask, *Which slope is it?* Help students make the same movement as the ball is making by passing their finger over the path the ball made. Then help them make the same movement on the slopes and see the one that has the same direction.

Engineering and arts – Make a craft slope.

Materials and preparation
- Glue
- Paper towel tubes (half per student, cut the tubes lengthwise in advance)
- Wrapping paper

Show students all the materials and tell them they are going to make a slope. Ask them if they can identify how to make it and what to use each of the materials for. Use their ideas to explain the procedures. Distribute the materials and have students make their slopes. Tell them not to glue wrapping paper inside the tube – as this might prevent anything from rolling down it.

When they have finished, have them compare their work with a classmate's and see if they have done anything differently.

DIFFERENTIATED INSTRUCTION

BELOW LEVEL
Science – Does it roll down?

Materials and preparation
- A selection of small objects such as crayons, marbles, erasers in different shapes, a key
- Students' craft slopes

In pairs, have students use small objects to test their slope and see what rolls and what doesn't. They can use crayons, marbles, erasers in different shapes, a key, etc.
Tell them to report the results to the class: *Marbles roll down.*

ABOVE LEVEL

Have students do the same procedures explained in *Below level*, but before having the objects roll down, tell them to make a guess if the object can or can't roll down and say why they think so. After checking, have them report the results to the class: *This eraser rolls down. This eraser doesn't. It's not round.*

> **Note to teachers**
> Students may realize that the objects that rolled down were round, but if they don't, you can help them understand it by grouping round objects and flat ones for them to see the differences more clearly.

CLOSING

Play *Up and down*. Say goodbye.

Materials and preparation
- Puppet

Have students stand up. Explain that they will play a game called *Up and down*. Ask them how the ball moved in the activities and have them gesture. As they do it, say *down*. Then point upwards and say *up*. Explain that every time you say *up* they should stand and when you say *down* they should crouch. You can also have a student give the instructions.
After that, say *goodbye* to students and have them say *goodbye* to you and the puppet.

Unit 5 How do you help at home?

Learning goals
- Measure objects using non-standard measuring tool
- Understand how big a house needs to be for differently-sized living things
- Relate tools and house chores
- Make a small broom for the little elf to help at home

STEAM subjects
- Arts
- Math

Thinking skills
Understanding, applying, analyzing, creating, evaluating

Main language content
What is it for? How can he help?
He can sweep the floor.
Adjectives: *big, small*
Words for household chores: *broom, clean, floor, house, sweep*
Animals: *birds, dogs, elephants, giraffes, hamsters*

OPENING

Circle time

Materials and preparation
- A bell
- Puppet
- Visual schedule pictures

Bring out the puppet and start by having it greet the students. After they greet the puppet, have the puppet greet you, too. Then elicit *hello* and ask students how they are today. Show them how to respond using their thumbs.

Hide the pictures representing today's schedule and have students look for them. Ask those who found the pictures to say what they will learn today. Help as needed.

Make the bell chime and ask, *Can you hear the chime?* Show a picture of one of today's activities and elicit, *It's (math) time!* Repeat with the other subject.

Math – What are the items for? Are they big?

Materials and preparation
- A broom
- A piece of cloth
- Dish soap

Have students sit in a circle and place the three items in the middle. Brainstorm with them ideas on what chores they can do around the house with the items that you have brought in.

After that, put two of the items next to each other, such as the broom and the dish soap bottle. Ask, *Which one is big? Which one is small?*

ACTIVE LEARNING

Arts and math – Look and draw a big or a small house.

Materials and preparation
- Big Book Unit 5: *The elves' house*
- Crayons or colored pencils
- Project Book page 37

Show students the pages of the story *The elves' house* and ask them if they can remember the story. Point to the pictures and elicit key elements, such as characters, their houses, and the chores the elves do. Help students open their Project Book to page 37. Tell them that in another place far, far away there lives a family of people. In their yard, there is a family of elves. Have students count the elves and the people.
Then say, *But where are their houses?* Tell students that they will draw the elves' and the people's houses. Ask, *Are the houses the same? Whose house is big? Whose house is small?* Help students understand that they need to draw a bigger house for the family and a smaller house for the elves. Monitor and help as needed.
Finally have students show their work to their classmates and say which house is big, which house is small, who lives in the big house, and who lives in the small house.

> **Note to teachers**
> Investigating and comparing objects and pictures in terms of size, length, etc. is a mathematical skill that should be developed from an early age. At first, students are likely to compare size by saying, for instance, *It's like my book*, which shows that this concept is being developed well.

Arts – Make a broom for the little elf to help.

Materials and preparation
- Big Book Unit 5: *The elves' house*
- Brown markers
- Brown paper cut into small triangles (one per student)
- Masking tape
- Wooden skewers

Show students the third page of the story and point to the little elf sitting at the table. Say, *This little elf helps at home, but he can't help sweep the floor. The broom is very big for him. How can we help?* Allow students to think of ways they can help the elves: they can make a small broom for him. Show students the materials. In small groups, have them think of ways to put the materials together and make a small broom. If necessary, show them the skewer and ask, *What part of the broom is this?* Repeat with the paper triangles and have them draw vertical lines in the triangle. Help them put the parts together using tape. While students are working, ask, *What do you use a broom for?* and help them with the answer.

DIFFERENTIATED INSTRUCTION

BELOW LEVEL
Math – Compare your broom with other objects.

Materials and preparation
- Students' craft brooms

Have students look for something as small as the broom they made. Then have everyone sit in a circle with their brooms and the objects. Ask one student at a time to place the objects next to each other to compare sizes. Encourage everyone to participate and check if the size is about the same.

ABOVE LEVEL

Have students look for something as small as the broom they made. Then divide students into pairs and ask them to compare their brooms with the objects they found. Have them work together to figure out which is bigger, the broom or the object they selected.

CLOSING

Talk about how big these animals' houses need to be. Say goodbye.

Tell students that you are going to tell them the name of different animals and they will think about the size of a house for this animal. If the animal is big, it needs a big house, so they will open their arms wide to show how big the house needs to be. They can also bring their hands close to show how small the house needs to be. Talk about *birds, dogs, elephants, giraffes, hamsters*.
Say *goodbye* to students and have them say *goodbye* back to you.

WHO CAN DO THESE CHORES? CIRCLE.

STEAM • HOW DO YOU HELP AT HOME? • UNIT 5 • 39

Learning goals
- Learn to use hand pointers in interactive games to make a choice
- Reflect on what household chores they can and can't do
- Understand that paper and food leftovers shouldn't go to the same trash can

STEAM subjects
- Science
- Technology

Thinking skills
Conceptualizing, analyzing, applying, evaluating, creating

Main language content
I can pick up toys. I can't cut fruits.
We can recycle paper. We can't recycle yogurt.
It's food. It isn't food.
Household chores: *cook, cut fruits and vegetables, pick up toys, separate garbage, take out the garbage, throw (paper) away*

OPENING

Circle time

Materials and preparation
- A bell
- Pieces of paper and some food leftovers (such as fruit peels, beet greens, and corncobs) in a bag
- Visual schedule pictures

Say *hello* to students as you enter the classroom and walk towards them throwing the garbage on the floor and pretending not to care. This will draw students' attention. Ask, *What's wrong?* and allow students to say how they feel about your action.
Ask for their help to put the items into the bag again, say *thank you*, and leave the bag aside.
Then place the visual schedule pictures face down in the circle. Call on a student to turn over a picture and show it to the rest of the class. Elicit the name of the subject. Make the bell chime and ask, *Can you hear the chime?* Elicit, *It's (science) time!* Repeat with the other subject.

Science – Learning about garbage

Materials and preparation
- Pieces of paper and some food leftovers (such as fruit peels, beet greens, and corncobs) in a bag

Take the garbage bag again and ask students if they liked it when you threw the garbage on the floor. Let them express how they felt freely.
Take out all the items and ask them if they all look the same. Ask, *How are they different?* If necessary, ask, *What is part of food here? What isn't part of food?* Elicit that paper is not part of this group. Tell students that paper can be used again after a machine makes it possible, but food leftovers can't.

ACTIVE LEARNING

Science – Help your family separate the garbage.

Materials and preparation
- Crayons (three sets)
- Paper balls (about twelve)
- Six baskets, three of which will have a green label

Show students two of the baskets, one of which will have a green label. Explain that here this label means that whatever is inside can be used again someday. Divide students into three groups and tell them that they will all be a family trying to separate their garbage. Show them a few crayons and say that they represent food leftovers, like a banana peel or an orange peel.

Give two baskets to each group and place the "garbage" in between. Explain that as you say *go*, they will separate the garbage, placing the paper in the green basket and the leftovers in the other basket. Say *go* and monitor the activity. When all groups finish, have all students check the other groups' garbage separation.

> **Note to teachers**
> When teaching about recycling and the correct disposal of garbage, it is always a good idea to include the leftovers and containers from students' snacks, as it helps them connect the idea of recycling to their own reality. You can also change the color green in the label for the color used in your school.

Technology – Who can do these chores? Circle.

Materials and preparation
- Project Book page 39
- Stickers

Help students open their Project Book to page 39. Say, *We can take out the garbage.* Ask, *What other chores do we do at home?* Tell students that the page shows a tablet and they need to circle the right person. Explain that they will choose who can do each of the chores and circle that person. Point to each picture and ask, *Who can do this chore, the boy or his daddy?* Monitor and help as needed.

DIFFERENTIATED INSTRUCTION

BELOW LEVEL
Technology – My own hand is a pointer.

Materials and preparation
- Flashcards: *banana*, *paper*
- Masking tape

Use tape to fix the flashcards on the wall within students' reach. Tell them to make a hand pointer (showing their index fingers and thumbs). Tell them that on computers we click using the index finger. Have them line up in front of the flashcards and tell students to "click" on what you tell them to. Say, for example, *Click on the banana!* and the student walks to the board and "clicks" on the banana flashcard. Give everyone a chance to play at least once.

ABOVE LEVEL

Do the procedures explained in *Below level*, but before students go to the end of the line, ask, *Can we recycle (bananas)?* and elicit *yes* or *no*.

CLOSING

Learn about separating your classroom garbage. Say goodbye.

Materials and preparation
- A pair of rubber gloves
- Classroom garbage can

Put on the rubber gloves and show students the classroom garbage. Remind them not to touch it themselves and ask, *Why am I wearing gloves?* Elicit that you are protecting your hands from germs. Show students what is in the garbage and have them say if it is paper, bottles, cans, or food leftovers. Have them check if the garbage in the can should all be together or should be separated. If it should be separated, elicit how.

After the discussion, tell students that it is time to say goodbye and say *bye* to them.

WHO SLEEPS IN EACH BED? LOOK AND CIRCLE.

STEAM • HOW DO YOU HELP AT HOME? • UNIT 5 • 41

Learning goals
- Compare and match items with the same length
- Develop spatial awareness
- Reflect on possible ways to help the elves clean the top glass windows
- Build a small ladder for the elves

STEAM subjects
- Engineering
- Math

Thinking skills
Remembering, understanding, applying, analyzing, creating, evaluating

Main language content
This is Grandpa's bed. This bed is too small. Are daddy and this bed the same size? Is the space big or small for you all? My ladder has four steps.
Family members: *baby, daddy, grandpa, sister*
Household chores: *clean the windows, make my bed*
Numbers: *1-6*

OPENING

Circle time

Materials and preparation
- A bell
- A book
- Puppet
- Visual schedule pictures

Say *hello* to students. Encourage them to say *hello* to you and the puppet. Make it answer, *Hello, my friends*. Then invite students to sit in a circle.
Cover the pictures of today's schedule using a book. Hold the pictures behind the book and show part of them only. Ask students if they can guess what activity it is. Repeat with the other picture. Show one picture at a time, make the bell chime, and ask, *Can you hear the chime?*
Elicit, *It's (engineering) time!* Repeat with the other subject.

Do you all fit in the square?

Materials and preparation
- Masking tape or chalk

Take students outside or make space in the classroom. Use tape or chalk to draw a square on the floor a little too small for all your students to stand inside. Ask everyone, *Is the space big or small for you all?* When all students have made a guess, have one at a time stand in the circle. When they are already crowded inside, ask again, *Is the space big or small for you all?* Help students understand that the space was too small for so many people.

ACTIVE LEARNING

Math – Who sleeps in each bed? Look and circle.

Materials and preparation
- Crayons
- Project Book page 41

Help students open their Project Book to page 41 and look at the elves. Ask, *Can you remember them? Who are they?* Point to each individual family member and ask, *Who is this?*
Then point to the first two family members and the bed. Ask, *Who sleeps in this bed?* Students should identify the size of the bed and who it belongs to. You can let them use their own hands to measure the size of each bed and elf.

> **Note to teachers**
> Sometimes simple daily chores can help students develop spatial awareness, such as putting away toys in a box or books on a shelf – both box and shelf size must be taken into consideration when they are putting things away.

How can we help the elf?

Materials and preparation
- Big Book Unit 5: *The elves' house*

Show students the second scene of the story they read a few lessons ago. Point to the elf who is cleaning the windows and say, *She cleans the windows. But look! These windows are very high! She can't clean the windows. How can we help?*
Allow students to think of and discuss ideas before presenting the craft materials.

Engineering and arts – Make a small ladder.

Materials and preparation
- Hot glue (teacher's use only) or masking tape
- Popsicle sticks (break a few of them in half beforehand)

Show students the popsicle sticks and the sticks cut in half. If nobody has come up with the idea of building a ladder, pretend to be trying to reach something very high in the classroom – so high that standing on a chair wouldn't do it – and ask students to consider how to help. Alternatively, you can also place two sticks together and place the first step.
Have students build their ladders and use tape to stick the steps to the poles. You can also use hot glue, but remember not to let students touch the glue.

DIFFERENTIATED INSTRUCTION

BELOW LEVEL
Math – Count steps and talk about a ladder size.

Materials and preparation
- Students' craft ladders

Divide students into pairs. Have them show each other their ladders and say if they are the same or different. Tell them to count the steps on it and say if their classmate's has the same number of steps.

ABOVE LEVEL

Have students do the procedures explained in *Below level*, but after that, tell them to think of a way to make their ladder higher without using any extra material other than a small piece of tape – they should reach the conclusion that by placing two or more ladders together, one on top of the other, they can make a higher one.

CLOSING

Play *I can!* and say goodbye.

Materials and preparation
- A student's craft ladder

Tell students to stand up. Every time you say something they can do, they should jump and say *I can!* Use gestures to help them understand. Start by holding a craft ladder and say, *Go up a ladder*. If students jump, tell them that going up a ladder is dangerous and they should ask for help when they need to take something that is out of their reach. Continue using sentences such as *clean the windows, pick up toys, cut fruits, sweep the floor.*
Finally, say *goodbye* to students and encourage them to reply.

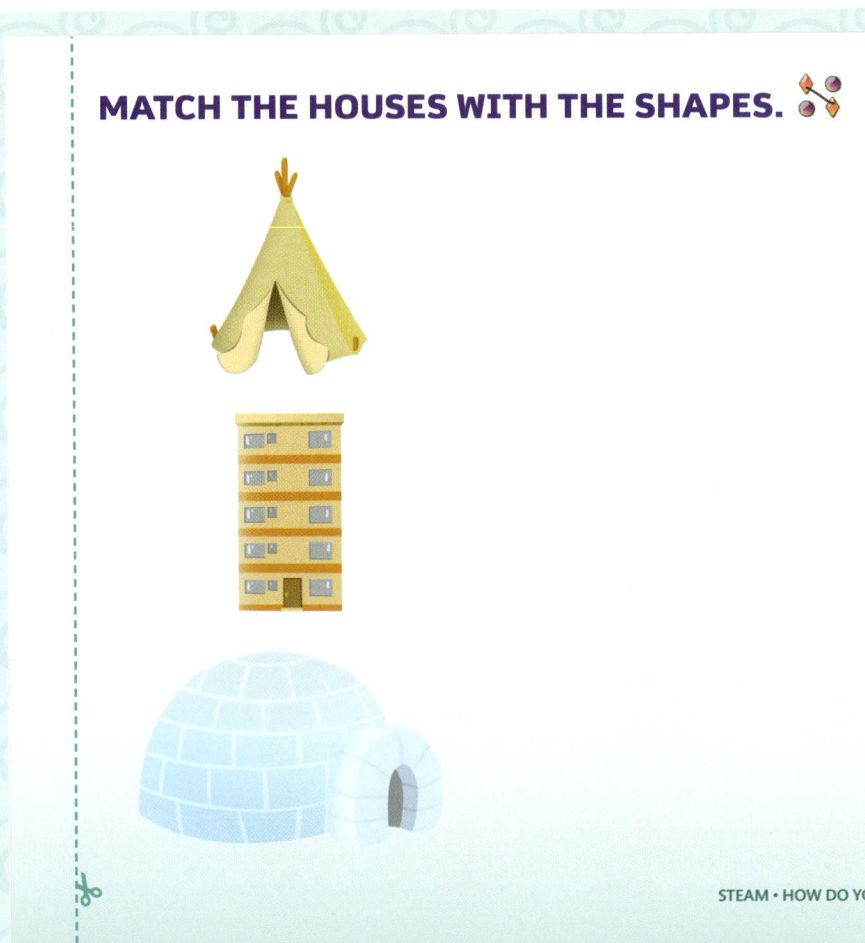

MATCH THE HOUSES WITH THE SHAPES.

STEAM • HOW DO YOU HELP AT HOME? • UNIT 5 43

Learning goals
- Learn that there are different kinds of houses
- Identify shapes in parts of the house
- Evaluate different tools to build a teepee

STEAM subjects
- Science
- Engineering
- Math

Thinking skills
Remembering, understanding, applying, analyzing, creating

Main language content
Where do (indigenous people) live? What color is the igloo?
Kinds of houses: *apartment, castle, house, hut, igloo, teepee*
Shapes: *circle, rectangle, square, triangle*

OPENING

Circle time

Materials and preparation
- A bell
- Puppet
- Visual schedule pictures

Greet students and have them greet you back. Ask, *How are you?* and have students show their thumbs up to respond.
Have them sit in a circle. Place the visual schedule pictures face down in the circle. Have two students turn them over and say what activity they represent. Make the bell chime and say, *Can you hear the chime?*
Show a picture of one of today's activities and elicit, *It's (engineering) time!* Repeat with the other subjects.

Kinds of houses

Materials and preparation
- House materials: fabric, ice cubes, leather, stone, straw
- Pictures of different kinds of houses from different cultures such as huts, igloos, teepees, etc. (print them out or project them)

Display the pictures of different types of houses and ask students what they are. Ask, *Is it a house?* Talk to students about houses being different in different cultures and countries. Talk about the materials each type of house is made of and bring some of that material to class (leather/fabric, stone, ice cubes, straw). Allow students to manipulate the material. Ask them to give their opinion on the questions, *Which material is stronger? Warmer? Cooler?*

ACTIVE LEARNING

Science – What is an igloo like?
Materials and preparation
- Picture of an igloo

Show students a picture of an igloo. Explain that in very cold places people make igloos to keep themselves warm. Igloos are made of blocks of ice. Students may think that this means that the igloo is really cold inside. However, it is important to explain that the thick blocks of ice block any winds and do not melt if there is heat inside the igloo. It is not uncommon to find igloos with hallways (just like in other built homes) that connect one igloo to the other.

Engineering and math – Match the houses with the shapes.
Materials and preparation
- Crayons
- Project Book page 43

Help students open their Project Book to page 43 and match the houses with the shapes they are related to. When correcting the activity, have students point to the shapes and say what they are as well as where in the houses they can see each shape. After that, ask, *Who lives in an igloo? Who lives in a teepee? Where do you live?*

Engineering – Make a teepee.
Materials and preparation
- A picture of a teepee
- Pieces of fabric
- Play dough
- String
- Toothpicks with the edges cut off

Tell students that teepees are Indigenous mobile homes that are set up by Indigenous women. The fabric used is canvas or buffalo skin. Challenge students to make a teepee using the materials provided. If necessary, help students structure their teepee by using play dough to keep the toothpicks together.

Note to teachers
Allowing students to imagine, plan, create, and experiment, which are tasks that are proposed in engineering activities, help them become better problem-solvers and develop innovative ideas.

DIFFERENTIATED INSTRUCTION

BELOW LEVEL
How are our houses the same?

Divide students into pairs. Have them talk about similarities in their houses. Give them a few ideas on what to talk about: color of their house outside, the rooms and their colors, and the things inside their bedroom. Have students share the similarities between their houses with the rest of the class.

ABOVE LEVEL

Have students do the same procedures explained in *Below level*, but have them also highlight differences between their houses. Have students share both the similarities and the differences between their houses with the rest of the class.

CLOSING

Do a gallery walk. Say goodbye.
Materials and preparation
- Puppet
- Students' craft teepee

Place all students' teepees around the classroom and have them do a gallery walk. Review the procedures for walking safely around the classroom and remind them not to crowd their classmates. Let students make comments on their classmates' work and how they like the work.
Then have everyone say *goodbye* to each other, to you, and the puppet.

Unit 6 How do you take care of your pet?

HELP THE SEAHORSE GET BACK TO THE SEA.

STEAM • HOW DO YOU TAKE CARE OF YOUR PET? • UNIT 6   45

Learning goals
- Learn about sea animals and their habitat
- Build the directions for the seahorse to get back to the sea
- Compare light and heavy objects
- Understand that lighter objects float in water

STEAM subjects
- Science
- Technology
- Arts
- Math

Thinking skills
Understanding, applying, analyzing, creating, evaluating

Main language content
Fish live in the sea. Fish swim.
Fish have fins. They don't have wings.
Is the shark floating?
Directions: *down, up*
Animals: *fish, puffer fish, seahorse, shark*

OPENING

Circle time

Materials and preparation
- A bell
- A book
- Puppet
- Visual schedule pictures

Say *hello* to students. Encourage them to say *hello* to you and the puppet. Make it answer, *Hello, my friends*. Then invite students to sit in a circle.

Cover the pictures of today's schedule using a book. Hold the pictures behind the book and only show part of them. Ask students if they can guess what activity it is. Repeat with the other pictures.

Show one picture at a time, make the bell chime, and ask, *Can you hear the chime?*

Elicit, *It's (technology) time!* Repeat with the other subjects.

Science – Sea animals

Materials and preparation
- Copies of the sea animals in the Student's Book (puffer fish, seahorse)
- Picture of a shark

Place the pictures in the circle face down. Tell students, *These are pictures of animals, but they don't live on land. Where do they live?* If necessary, help students by pretending that you are swimming and making waves with your hands.

Invite three students to turn over the pictures and ask all students what sea animals they are.

48   STEAM

ACTIVE LEARNING

Technology and math – Help the seahorse get back to the sea.

Materials and preparation
- Project Book page 45
- Unit 6 stickers

Help students open their Project Book to page 45. Point to the seahorse and ask, *What animal is this? Is it in the correct place? Do seahorses live on land?* Ask students where seahorses live and have them find the sea in the picture. Then say, *Let's help the seahorse get back to the sea.* Encourage them to use their finger to follow the correct path to the sea. Then have students peel off the stickers showing arrows and place them in the correct path from the seahorse to the sea. Remind them that the seahorse must go down the path and show an arrow pointing down. Show an arrow pointing up and show disapproval for them to understand it is the wrong direction here. Monitor and help as needed.
Allow students to compare their work with a classmate's before checking as a class.

> **Note to teachers**
> When teaching students about a path made or followed by arrows, you are both helping them develop their sense of direction and understand that a set of instructions can help an object perform a task, which is the foundation for learning about algorithms.

Science and arts – Make shark balloons.

Materials and preparation
- Black markers
- Pictures of a shark and of a bone
- Syringe
- Two balloons
- Water

Show students the shark. Ask students if they can see sharks in the water or if they only live in the deep sea. Help them understand that it is often possible to see sharks as they float.
Ask students if they know what bones are. Use the picture of the bone for them to remember what it is. Say, *Our bones are heavy* (gesture as you say this), *but shark's bones are light* (gesture again). *The water is heavy. The bones are light.* Move your hand down for heavy and up for light and make them meet to show that light goes above heavy.
Tell students that they are going to do an experiment. Ask for their help to blow up one of the balloons with air and tie a knot to close it. Fill the other balloon with a little water. You can invite a student to help and use the syringe. As both balloons are tied off, tell students they are sharks. Say, *Let's draw faces on the shark. How many eyes? How are the teeth? Let's draw sharp teeth.* Invite different students to collaborate.
Ask students to guess which one will float and which one will sink. Take notes of their answers on the board using tally marks.

DIFFERENTIATED INSTRUCTION

BELOW LEVEL
Science – Which balloon can float? Let's find out!

Materials and preparation
- Bucket or bowl with water
- Shark balloons from previous activity

Have students sit in a circle. Tell them to pass around the balloons, both of them together, and say which one they need more strength to hold (the water balloon). Then invite a student to put both in the water and ask, *Is the water shark floating? Is the air shark floating?* Remind students that air is light, so this shark floats.

ABOVE LEVEL

Have students sit in a circle. Tell them to pass around the balloons, both of them together, and say how different they feel. Allow them to give their opinion freely. If necessary, hold the balloons yourself and pretend that one of them is way heavier than the other. Ask, *Which one?* and elicit, *The water (balloon/shark).*
Then invite a student to put both in the water and ask, *Is the water shark floating? Is the air shark floating?* Ask students why they think the water shark sinks, but the air shark doesn't. Help them understand that air is lighter than water, so it stays on top of the water.

> **Note to teachers**
> If you have both *Below* and *Above level* groups working at the same time, duplicate the balloons.

CLOSING

Compare different sea animals. Say goodbye.

Materials and preparation
- Copies of the sea animals in the Student's Book (puffer fish, seahorse)
- Picture of a shark
- Puppet

Ask students to describe the animals in the pictures. Then ask, *Can sea animals fly? Why not?* Help students understand that sea animals don't have wings, they have fins that help them swim. Then have students compare the animals in terms of size and color.
Then say *goodbye* to all the students and encourage them to say *goodbye* back. Have them also say *goodbye* to the puppet and use its animal name: *Goodbye, puffer fish!*

Unit 6 | 49

Learning goals
- Understand what a pet fish needs to live well
- Make a craft puffer fish
- Use play dough to take the puffer fish to the sea

STEAM subjects
- Science
- Engineering
- Arts

Thinking skills
Understanding, applying, analyzing

Main language content
It's round. It's thin.
It's brown. It's pink.
They aren't big. They're small.
Don't tap on the tank.
Pet fish needs: *food, tank, water*

OPENING

Circle time

Materials and preparation
- A bell
- A book
- Puppet
- Visual schedule pictures

Say *hello* to students. Encourage them to say hello to you and the puppet. Make it answer, *Hello, my friends*. Then invite students to sit in a circle.
Cover the pictures of today's schedule using a book. Hold the pictures behind the book and show part of them only. Ask students if they can guess what activity it is. Repeat with the other pictures.
Show one picture at a time, make the bell chime, and ask, *Can you hear the chime?*
Elicit, *It's (engineering) time!* Repeat with the other subjects.

Play *Run and tap the picture*.

Materials and preparation
- Copies of the sea animals from the Student's Book (puffer fish and seahorse)
- Masking tape
- Picture of a shark

Use tape to place the pictures on the wall within students' reach. Have them line up facing the pictures. Give students clues and have them tap the correct picture. Give them clues that match both fish as well and tell them to tap both. Say, for example, *It lives in the sea. It's round. It's thin. It's pink. It's brown. It swims.* You can repeat clues, so make sure all students get to tap the pictures at least once.

ACTIVE LEARNING

Science – What does a pet fish need to live? Circle.

Materials and preparation
- Crayons or pencils
- Project Book page 47

Help students open their Project Book to page 47 and look at the pictures. First have them look at the fish and ask, *What animal is this? Does it live in the sky, water, or on land?* Then ask, *Does anyone here have a pet fish?*

If a student or two respond affirmatively, ask them what it is like to have a pet fish, *Can you take it out of the water? What does it need? Does it need food to live? Does it need clean water?* If nobody has a pet fish, have students guess the answers to the questions.

Tell students to look at the other pictures. Explain that they will circle the pictures that show what a pet fish needs to live. Allow them to do the activity alone and then compare with a classmate. When correcting the activity, ask about each of the items, *Do fish need (water) to live? Can you tap on the tank? Don't tap on the tank. It scares them.*

Arts – Make a puffer fish.

Materials and preparation
- Brushes
- Glue
- Pink and black paint
- Pink triangle cutouts made out of crepe paper
- Styrofoam balls
- Wooden skewers (make sure both ends are blunt)

Give students a foam ball and help them stick a wooden skewer in it in order to hold the fish while painting it. Say, *We are going to make a puffer fish! What color is it?* Have students paint it pink. Then ask, *How can puffer fish see?* Elicit that they have eyes and encourage students to use black paint to draw the eyes on it. Help as needed. Finally ask, *How can it swim?* Help students remember that fish have fins and they need the fins to swim. Give them the triangle cutouts and teach them how to glue one end of the triangle on the right and left side of the fish.

Encourage students to show their puffer fish to their classmates and talk about its features: *two eyes, fins,* etc. Ask them to talk about its color, too.

DIFFERENTIATED INSTRUCTION

BELOW LEVEL
Engineering – Make the puffer fish go to the sea.

Materials and preparation
- Light blue circles
- Play dough or clay
- Student's puffer fish

First make a straight path out of play dough or clay. Ask a student to try to roll their puffer fish along the path. The puffer fish will probably roll off before it reaches the other end. Invite a student to show the path it really followed with their finger. Then ask, *How can we make it roll to the end?* Then tell students, *Help me with your hands!* Have them put their hands on the sides of the path so that when the fish rolls off the path, their hands can hold it. After that, make a few more paths and have students work in pairs to build a barrier on the sides of the path so that the puffer fish reaches the sea. Place a light blue circle at the end of each path to pretend it is the sea the fish needs to get to and have them try to roll it along the way.

ABOVE LEVEL

Do the first step in *Below level*. Listen to students' ideas on how to make the ball roll to the end and help them reach the conclusion that the path needs something to protect the sides so the fish doesn't roll off. Give them play dough and tell them to think of a way to protect the sides. Have them make a few trials and encourage them to keep trying. When a pair comes up with a solution, have them show it to the others so that everyone can try. Finally place a light blue circle at the end of the path to pretend it is the sea the fish needs to get to and have them try to roll it along the way.

CLOSING

Play with your fish while singing the *Goodbye song*.

Materials and preparation
- Audio library - songs
- Students' puffer fish

Invite students to choose a spot and play with their pet fish together with their classmates. Meanwhile, play the *Goodbye song* (track 05). Walk around and ask them to pretend their fish is swimming in the sea. Have them make wavy movements with the fish.

Say *goodbye* to your students and have them say *goodbye* back to you

> **Note to teachers**
>
> For their next STEAM class, ask students to bring a stuffed animal to school. Prepare a few stuffed animals in case some students forget theirs.

DRAW THE STEPS TO MAKE YOUR PET'S SLEEPING PLACE.

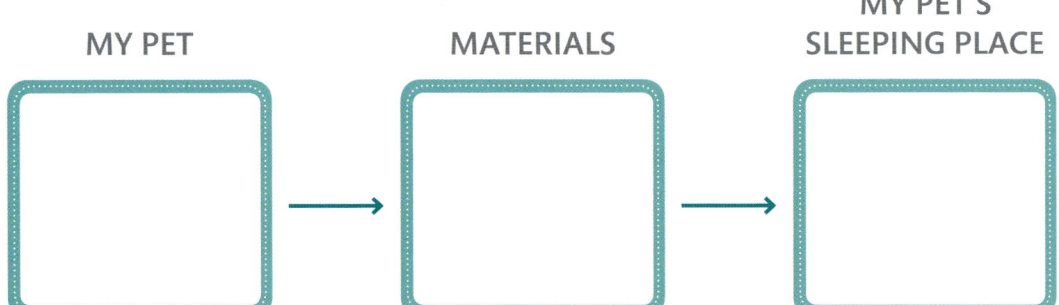

MY PET → MATERIALS → MY PET'S SLEEPING PLACE

STEAM • HOW DO YOU TAKE CARE OF YOUR PET? • UNIT 6 • 49

Learning goals
- Talk about how they take care of pets
- Understand that animals sleep in different ways
- Build a bed for a pet

STEAM subjects
- Science
- Engineering
- Arts
- Math

Thinking skills
Remembering, understanding, applying, analyzing, creating

Main language content
It's a teddy bear.
It has two eyes.
It's a (cat). My pet's name is (Bob).
I give food to my pet. I take my pet for a walk.
I help change the water in the tank.
Pets: *bird, cat, dog, fish, hamster, parrot, turtle*

OPENING

Circle time

Materials and preparation
- A bell
- Puppet
- Visual schedule pictures

Bring out the puppet and start by having it greet the students. After they greet the puppet, have the puppet greet you, too. Then elicit *Hello!* and ask students how they are today.
Hide the pictures representing today's schedule and have students look for them. Then place them in the circle. Make the bell chime and ask, *Can you hear the chime?* Ask students if they remember how to reply and help as needed.
Show a picture of one of today's activities and elicit, *It's (science) time!* Repeat with the other subjects.

Science – Talk about your pet and what a pet needs.

Materials and preparation
- Students' stuffed animals

Ask students to pretend that the stuffed animal they brought is their pet and have them present it to their classmates. Help by asking questions, *What's its name? What animal is it? What color is it?* Encourage students to say something about it such as about its size and color, who gave the stuffed toy to them, if it is special to them and why.
Then ask the whole class, *How do you take care of pets? What do pets need?* Have students list things pets need. Mime eating, sleeping, walking, or playing to help students understand some basic needs of most pets.

> **Note to teachers**
> When working with presentations, it is important to set students' expectations and remind them to respect each other's speaking time.

ACTIVE LEARNING

Engineering and arts – Make a sleeping place for your pet.

Materials and preparation

- Assorted materials you may have at your disposal to build a bed for a pet. Suggestions: building blocks, clay, cotton, pieces of fabric, old newspapers, tape, popsicle sticks, straws, transparent plastic cups
- Brushes
- Glue
- Masking tape
- Paint
- Students' stuffed animals

Elicit the names of the pets they have seen in the previous activity and encourage students to talk about where these pets sleep. Ask, *What kind of bed does a (dog) have? Is it similar to your own bed? Do all animals sleep in beds? Where do fish sleep?* Next show the materials you have available (building blocks, sticks, straws, fabric, etc.) and ask students to think how they could use these materials to make a sleeping place for these pets. You can first brainstorm as a whole class. For example, if they choose a dog, they can make a cotton bed on popsicle sticks taped together; if they choose a fish, they can make a tank using a transparent plastic cup and painting it light blue to pretend it is the water inside; if they choose a bird, like a parrot, they can use popsicle sticks to make a perch. Let them be creative and think of solutions that are practical for the animal they chose.

> **Note to teachers**
> When working with both arts and engineering, it is important to help students balance their creativity with effective design of whatever they are supposed to build. Make sure to help them reach this balance in a healthy way.

DIFFERENTIATED INSTRUCTION

BELOW LEVEL
Engineering and math – Draw the steps to make your pet's sleeping place.

Materials and preparation

- Crayons or pencils
- Project Book page 49

Help students open their Project Book to page 49. Tell students that the three boxes in the page will show today's project. Say, *In the first box, let's draw our pet.* Wait for them to finish, then say, *In the last box, let's draw the sleeping place we made: the dog bed, the fish tank, the bird perch.* Finally ask, *What comes in between?* Have students draw the step between these two: the materials they used to build their pet's sleeping place.
Talk about each of the steps in order and have students point to them. Then talk about the steps in a random order and have students point to them as you say the steps.

ABOVE LEVEL
Have students do the procedures explained in *Below level*, but after they have finished drawing, invite them to describe and point to the steps in order. Help them with the language as needed.

CLOSING

Present your pet's sleeping place. Say goodbye.

Materials and preparation

- Students' pet's sleeping place craft

Divide students into two groups and have them sit in circles. Tell them to show their craft to their classmates saying what pet it is, where it sleeps, and what materials they used to make the bed. Help them with language as needed.
Then have everyone shake hands with their classmates in the same group and say *goodbye*. Say *goodbye* to them yourself.

Learning goals
- Practice one-to-one correspondence
- Group animals according to the way they sleep
- Make a sleeping place that fits more than one pet

STEAM subjects
- Arts
- Math

Thinking skills
Remembering, understanding, applying, analyzing, creating

Main language content
What pet is it? Where does the dog live?
How many pets in this house?
In this house, there are six birds.
Pets: *bird, cat, dog, fish, hamster*
Numbers: *1-6*
Pets: *bird, cat, dog, fish, hamster, parrot, turtle*

OPENING

Circle time

Materials and preparation
- A bell
- Puppet
- Visual schedule pictures

Greet students and have them greet you back. Ask, *How are you?* and have students show their thumbs up to respond.
Have them sit in a circle. Place the visual schedule pictures face down in the circle. Have two students turn them over and say what activity they represent. Make the bell chime and say, *Can you hear the chime?*
Show a picture of one of today's activities and elicit, *It's (math) time!* Repeat with the other subject.

Remembering animal needs

Still sitting in a circle, have students talk about what they remember of the needs animals have. If they have pets, have them relate to the needs of their own pets. If they don't come up with these ideas, pretend to be eating, sleeping, or playing and have students say what animals do.
Finally ask, *Do birds and dogs sleep in the same way? Do rabbits and fish sleep in the same way?* Allow students to give their opinion freely. If any students have birds or fish, ask them if they have seen these animals sleeping and how they were.
Tell students they will find out about this later in today's class.

ACTIVE LEARNING

Math – Group pets in the same house.

Materials and preparation

- Pictures from magazines or printouts of different pets – more than one copy of each pet

Have students remain sitting in a circle. Place the pictures in the middle of the circle and have them name the animals. Say, *In this town, all birds live in the same house. All dogs live in the same house, too.* Invite students to group the pictures according to the animal and the house where they live. Then have them say, *In this house, there are (four) dogs.*

Which pets sleep on a bed? Circle green. Which animals don't lie down to sleep? Circle blue.

Materials and preparation

- Blue and green crayons
- Pictures of a bird and a fish sleeping (this last one, just a fish in a tank with eyes open)
- Project Book page 51

Help students open their Project Book to page 51 and look at the animals. Ask, *What pets are these? Does anyone here have a (hamster) at home?* Have students take a green crayon. Say, *Some animals lie down to sleep, they sleep on a bed. Can you circle these animals?* Have everyone say what animals they have circled. Then have them take the blue crayon and circle those animals that don't lie down to sleep – the bird and the fish. Help students understand that fish usually don't have eyelids so they don't close their eyes and they look as if they were awake when they are sleeping.

DIFFERENTIATED INSTRUCTION

BELOW LEVEL
Arts and math – Put all the pets in a house.

Materials and preparation

- Brushes
- Egg cartons cut in half (make sure to have six cups each half)
- Glue
- Paint
- Small pictures of pets: a bird, a cat, a dog, a hamster, a rabbit, a turtle (one set per student)

Divide students into pairs. Give them half an egg carton, a set of animals, and glue. Say, *These cups are houses. Pets live in these houses. There is one pet in each house. How many pets in this house?* Point to one of the cups and elicit, *One.* Have students choose an animal to glue in that cup. Ask about the second cup, too. From the third cup on, say, *I bet you know how many animals are here. And here?* Make sure students understand the one-to-one correspondence between the houses and the pets.
Have pairs compare their work with another pair of classmates. Have them also see if they have coincidently chosen the same place to glue an animal.

ABOVE LEVEL

Give students half an egg carton, a set of animals, and glue. Say, *These cups are houses. Pets live in this house. All houses have pets. Let's count the houses!* Have students count to six. *Let's count the pets.* Have students count to six, again. Then have students discuss as a whole group how many pets they can put in each house to make sure all houses have one pet. Let them try to divide it for a while before you intervene. After a while, help them see that there might be a house with no pets and one with two, for example.
Finally allow students to decorate their houses as they like.

CLOSING

Play *Clap for the same*. Say goodbye.

Materials and preparation

- Students' egg carton pet houses

Have students sit in a circle with their pet houses. Invite three or four students, one at a time, to talk about what animal they put in each house. If their classmate has the same dog in the same house, have them clap. Monitor and check if they are clapping at the correct moment.
Then have students say *goodbye* to you and to the puppet. Say *goodbye* to them, too.

Unit 7 What is your favorite food?

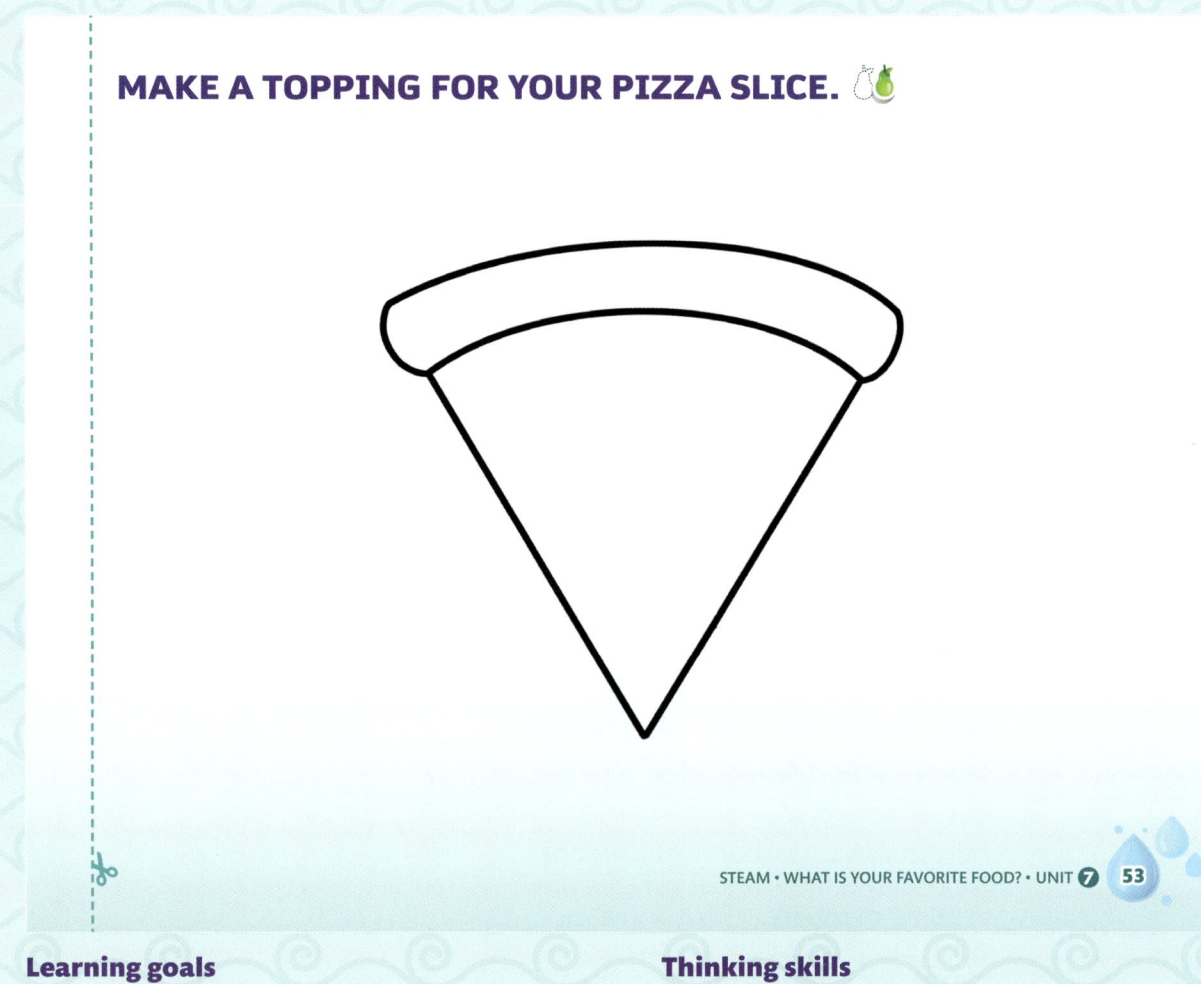

MAKE A TOPPING FOR YOUR PIZZA SLICE.

STEAM • WHAT IS YOUR FAVORITE FOOD? • UNIT 7 • 53

Learning goals
- Make slices of pizza
- Understand fractions by putting pieces together to form a whole
- Practice grouping food items

STEAM subjects
- Arts
- Math

Thinking skills
Remembering, understanding, applying, analyzing, creating

Main language content
I have one. We have six.
Too many! You need more.
Food: *apple, banana, cheese, chocolate, olives, orange, pizza*
Colors: *brown, green, orange, red, yellow*
Numbers: *1-6*

OPENING

Circle time

Materials and preparation
- A bell
- Puppet
- Visual schedule pictures

Bring out the puppet and start by having it greet the students. After they greet the puppet, have the puppet greet you, too. Then elicit *Hello!* and ask students how they are today. Show them how to respond using their thumbs.

Hide the pictures representing today's schedule and have students look for them. Ask those who found the pictures to say what they will learn today. Help as needed.

Make the bell chime and ask, *Can you hear the chime?* Show a picture of one of today's activities and elicit, *It's (math) time!* Repeat with the other subject.

Math – Play the *Fruit salad game.*

Gather students around in a circle and divide them into three groups. Have groups choose a fruit to name their group, such as *apple*, and get together, one next to the other, but still as part of a single circle. Place a student inside the circle. The student who is inside calls out the name of one of the groups and all the students who belong to this group need to get up quickly and exchange places themselves.

After the game, ask, *How many (apples)?* and have students count how many classmates there are in their fruit group.

56 STEAM

ACTIVE LEARNING

Math – Learn about fractions and dividing fruits.

Materials and preparation
- Cutting board
- Fresh fruit, such as an apple or a banana
- Paring knife (teacher's use only)
- Puppet

Tell students that today they are going to learn about dividing something into parts to give a part to everyone and about taking only a piece of something, a part of something that is whole.

Show students a fruit and say, *I have this banana. It's one banana only. I want banana and the puppet wants banana, too. But I have only one. What can I do?* Allow students to think about sharing what they have and help them understand that dividing the banana into two parts is a good idea. Then say, *One part for me and one part for you, (puppet's name).*

Take another fruit and cut it into two parts. Show them to students and have them count, *one, two*. Then cut the two parts in half and tell students you have quarters now, and count, *One, two, three, four.* Explain the importance of dividing things and sharing with others. Ask, *What do you share with others? A pizza? A fruit?* Finally say that, when we divide equally, everyone gets the same quantity or a piece of the same size.

> **Note to teachers**
> When working with tools that can't be handled by students, make sure to remind them that they can't use that tool. When working with toothpicks, remind students to be careful so as not to hurt themselves.

> **Note to teachers**
> Remember to check with parents for allergies before offering any food to students.

Arts – Make a topping for your pizza slice.

Materials and preparation
- Crayons
- Glue
- Leaves or grass
- Project Book page 53
- Scissors (teacher's use only)
- Small colored paper cutouts: *circles, ovals, squares, triangles*

Help students open their Project Book to page 53. Tell them to look at the picture and guess what it is. If necessary, give them some clues: *You eat this. It's delicious. It's not an everyday food, it's a sometimes food.* Then have everyone say the word *pizza*. Ask, *What's missing? This pizza doesn't look delicious.* If students answer in L1, repeat after them using English, *topping*.
Tell students that they are going to make their own pizza slice. Have them brainstorm what they could put on their pizza and help them with the language.
Then show them the materials available and ask them to think of ways they could use it to make their pizza slice. As they work, walk around and ask them what is on their pizza and what colors they see. When they finish, tell them to tell a classmate what there is on their pizza.

> **Note to teachers**
> As you walk around, cut out a pizza slice for each student.

DIFFERENTIATED INSTRUCTION

BELOW LEVEL
Math – Use your pizza slice to make a whole pizza.

Materials and preparation
- A few pizza slices decorated by yourself (as many as you need to form a multiple of six in the number of pizza slices in the classroom)
- Students' pizza slice

Tell students to get together in groups of six. Have them all say how many slices of pizza they have in one hand, *I have one slice.* Then have them think of a way to put all the slices together and form a whole pizza. Let students figure out how to do this by themselves before interfering.
When they have all been able to form a pizza, have students count how many slices the whole pizza has and then explain to them, *Six slices of pizza makes a whole pizza!*

ABOVE LEVEL

Tell students that they are going to put their slice of pizza together with other classmates' to make a whole pizza. Tell them to work in groups, but don't say how many in each group, and allow them to group themselves alone. If they notice that there are too many slices or too few, help them understand that they should reconsider the number of slices. *Seven is too many! Only four? You need more.*
When they have all been able to form a pizza, have students count how many slices the whole pizza has and then explain to them, *Six slices of pizza makes a whole pizza!*

CLOSING

Sing the *Goodbye song*.

Materials and preparation
- Audio library – songs

Play the *Goodbye song* (track 05) and pause after a while. Ask students questions to review what they learned today, for example, *How many slices in our whole pizza? (Student's name), what did you put on your pizza slice? (Puppet's name) and I want to eat the banana, but I only have one banana. What can we do? How many parts do we need?* Pause the song as many times as the number of questions you have. Then play the whole song and wave goodbye to students.

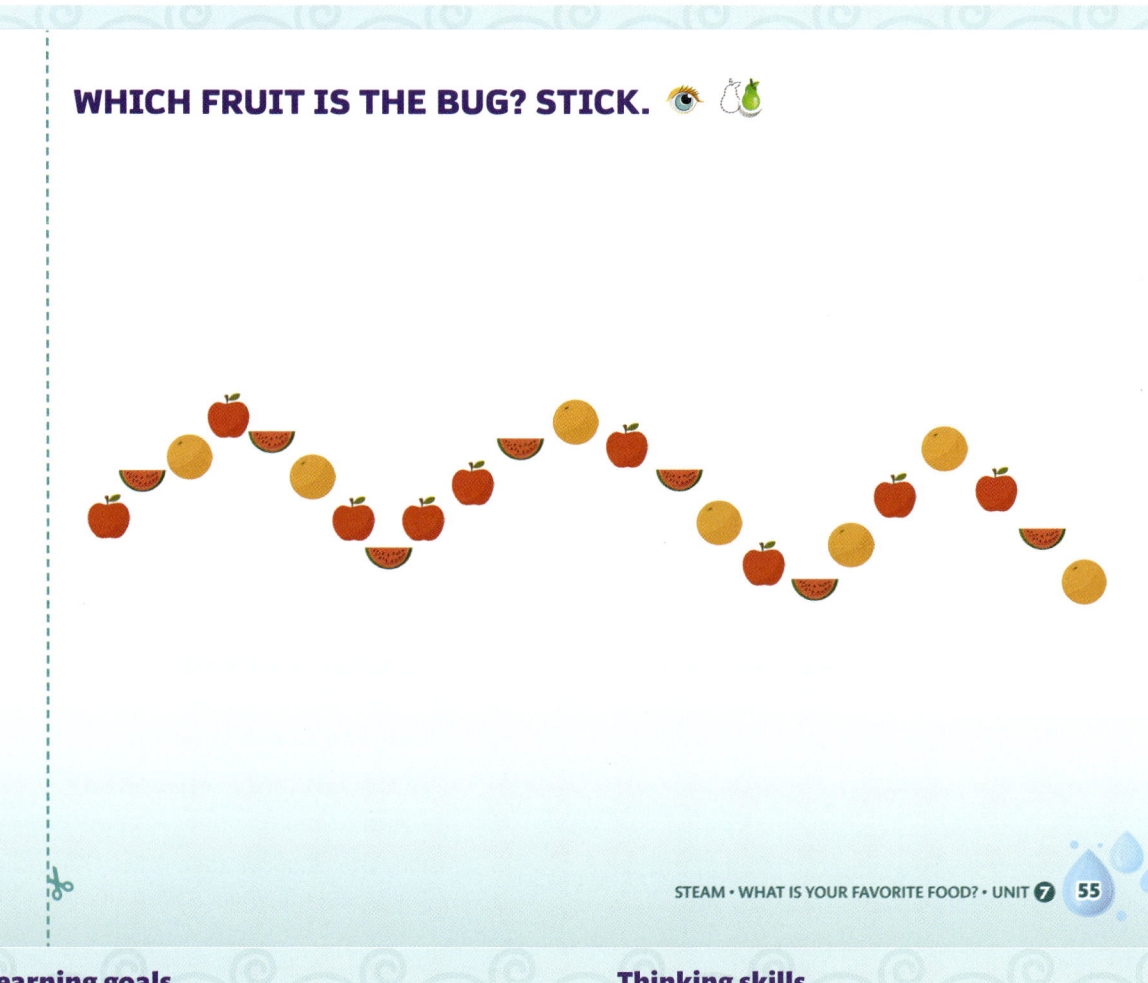

Learning goals
- Learn about where fruits come from
- Understand that some fruits grow on trees, and others in the ground or on bushes
- Plan the development of an idea and understand the meaning of *bug*

STEAM subjects
- Science
- Technology

Thinking skills
Remembering, conceptualizing, applying, analyzing

Main language content
Where is the bug?
Apples come from trees.
Watermelons grow in the ground.
Fruits: *apple, lemon, orange, watermelon*
Numbers: *1-6*

OPENING

Circle time

Materials and preparation
- A bell
- A book
- Puppet
- Visual schedule pictures

Say *hello* to students. Encourage them to say *hello* to you and the puppet. Make it answer, *Hello, my friends.* Then invite students to sit in a circle.
Cover the pictures of today's schedule using a book. Hold the pictures behind the book and show part of them only. Ask students if they can guess what activity it is. Repeat with the other picture.
Show one picture at a time, make the bell chime, and ask, *Can you hear the chime?*
Elicit, *It's (technology) time!* Repeat with the other subject.

Technology – What is a bug?

Materials and preparation
- A copy of the computer bug sticker
- A small red piece of paper
- Small blue pieces of paper (one per student)

Show students the picture of the bug. Ask them if they know what animal it is. Say *bug* and have them repeat. Then explain to students that the word *bug* is also used to talk about mistakes in computer programs that cause them to have problems functioning. Give each student a piece of blue paper and give one student at random a red piece of paper. Have everyone show their paper to their classmates. Say, *This is a computer game. It's the blue computer game. But wait, there is a bug! One piece of paper is not blue. Where is it?* Have students identify who has a red piece of paper and say, *Here is the bug!* Ask that student to leave the circle for a while and say, *Now the game is OK.*

Invite the student to go back to the circle and redistribute the pieces of paper, having students identify the bug in the blue computer game by themselves.

> **Note to teachers**
> A computer or system bug is a fault in the system of instructions that operates a computer. When a system or program is designed, it is expected to perform in a certain way. When mistakes happen and it fails to perform that way, this failure is called a bug.

ACTIVE LEARNING

Technology – Which fruit is the bug? Stick.

Materials and preparation
- Project Book page 55
- Unit 7 stickers

Help students open their Project Book to page 55. Have them name the three fruits on the page. Then say, *This is the plan for a computer game. It's a fruit game. The game always shows an apple, a watermelon, an orange.* Say the fruits again and have them point. Then say, *There are two bugs in this game. Let's find them!* Have students chant *apple, watermelon, orange, apple, watermelon, orange...* Continue the chant, but this time point to the pictures as they say it. When they reach the apple in the place of a watermelon, pretend to be confused. Say, *Wait. Is this correct? What is the correct fruit here?* Have students identify that this is the flaw in the order of the elements and have them peel off a bug sticker and place it on the fruit that is incorrect.

Then allow students to look for the second bug by themselves. Monitor and help as needed.

> **Note to teachers**
> Teaching students to identify elements that don't belong in a sequence is a great way to introduce the logical organization of systems and how diverting from this organization can influence the system as a whole.

Science – Where does fruit come from?

Materials and preparation
- Pictures of a lemon tree, an orange tree, an apple tree, and a watermelon on the ground

Have students remain sitting in a circle. Ask, *Do you know where oranges come from?* Allow students to expose their ideas and show reactions according to how close they get to the correct answer.

Display the tree pictures and ask students if they can identify the tree and its fruit. Ask, *Can you see this tree in your town? Do you like this fruit? Do all fruits come from trees?* After asking the last question and listening to students' answers, show them the picture of a watermelon on the ground and ask again, having them check their answers. Finally explain that some fruits come from trees, some grow in the ground, and some grow on bushes.

> **Note to teachers**
> Students tend to relate questions they are asked to their own experiences, so if they answer, for instance, that fruits come from the market or supermarket, make sure to highlight that they can find fruits there and help them think about the place where the fruit was before.

DIFFERENTIATED INSTRUCTION

BELOW LEVEL
Play *Tree or ground*.

Tell students that they are going to play a game and have them stand up. If possible, take them outside. Call on two students to be a tree and the ground. Say, *How does a tree look?* Have that student pretend to be a tree. Then invite the other student to lie on the floor and pretend to be the ground. Tell the other students that you will call out names of fruits and they will run to the tree or the ground according to where the fruit grows. Have different students play the tree and the ground.

ABOVE LEVEL
Play *Guess what fruit I am*.

Tell students that they are going to play a game and have them stand up. If possible, take them outside. Call on two students to be a tree and the ground. Say, *What does a tree look like?* Have that student pretend to be a tree. Then invite the other student to lie on the floor and pretend to be the ground. Whisper the name of a fruit in each student's ear, including fruits that grow on trees or bushes and in the ground. Tell students that when you say, *Fruits, go!* they need to run to the correct place, for example, if they are a fruit that grows on a tree, they run to the tree. Then have the student who is a tree and the student who is the ground guess which fruits their classmates are. Play the game more than once.

CLOSING

Find the bugs. Say goodbye.

Have a student leave the classroom for a while or ask them to cover their eyes. Take six students and have them make a line facing the board. Choose one of the students in the line to turn around and face the class. Call the student back and have them count the number of classmates they see and say where the bug is.

Have different students play and create different patterns.

Then say *goodbye* to students and encourage them to say *goodbye* back to you.

WHICH PICTURE IS MISSING FROM THE PUZZLE? LOOK AND CIRCLE.

STEAM • WHAT IS YOUR FAVORITE FOOD? • UNIT 7   57

Learning goals
- Learn to put pieces of a puzzle together
- Make an orange tree
- Think of ways to improve the tree to hold more oranges

STEAM subjects
- Engineering
- Arts
- Math

Thinking skills
Remembering, understanding, applying, analyzing, creating, evaluating, improving

Main language content
It's a puzzle.
It has ten pieces.
It's an orange tree.
Five oranges.
Fruits: *apple, banana, orange, pineapple, watermelon*
Numbers: *1-10*

OPENING

Circle time

Materials and preparation
- A bell
- A book
- Puppet
- Visual schedule pictures

Say *hello* to students. Encourage them to say *hello* to you and the puppet. Make it answer, *Hello, my friends*. Then invite students to sit in a circle.
Cover the pictures of today's schedule using a book. Hold the pictures behind the book and show part of them only. Ask students if they can guess what activity it is. Repeat with the other picture. Show one picture at a time, make the bell chime, and ask, *Can you hear the chime?*
Elicit, *It's (engineering) time!* Repeat with the other subjects.

Math – Put the puzzle together. What fruit is it?

Materials and preparation
- Pictures of an apple, a banana, an orange, a pineapple, and a watermelon cut into square pieces (about six pieces in all)

Divide the students into five groups and give each group a set of cutouts that form a fruit. Have them try to guess what fruit it is before starting. Then have students put the puzzle together and check if they guessed correctly.

> **Note to teachers**
> Besides developing students' fine motor skills, solving puzzles is a great way to help them develop their spatial awareness and problem-solving skills.

ACTIVE LEARNING

Math – Which picture is missing from the puzzle? Look and circle.

Materials and preparation
- Crayons or pencils
- Project Book page 57

Help students open their Project Book to page 57. Show them the puzzle and have them say what they see. Then encourage them to count the pieces. Say, *Wait, where is piece number ten?* Have students look at the two pieces on the right and identify the one that fits the blank. Encourage them to explain their choice. If necessary, help them identify that part of the pineapple is already showing, so they need the rest of the pineapple. If students choose the apple, point to the part of the pineapple that is already in the puzzle and ask, *What fruit is this? And where is the rest?*

Arts – Make an orange tree.

Materials and preparation
- Cardboard tubes
- Glue
- Green crepe paper
- Leaves and sticks
- Orange pompoms
- Play dough
- Popsicle sticks

Allow time for students to check the material available. Ask them, *How can you use this material to build a tree?* Allow students to think and exchange ideas. Ask, *What are the different parts of a tree?* Elicit, *The trunk, branches, and fruit.* If students use L1 or just describe the parts, repeat after them using the correct term in English. Have students use the material to make their tree. Monitor and help as needed. Students can use either the cardboard tubes or popsicle sticks as the trunk. They can use the crepe paper, the leaves, or the play dough to make the crown.

DIFFERENTIATED INSTRUCTION

BELOW LEVEL
Engineering – Make your tree hold more oranges.

Materials and preparation
- Glue
- Orange pompons
- Play dough
- Students' craft trees

Divide students into small groups. Ask, *How can you improve your tree to hold more oranges?* Take two different orange trees, one of them having the crown made of play dough. Ask students to help you put more oranges on the tree. They will notice that the oranges can stay on the play dough, but they might make the crepe paper fall if there are too many oranges. Invite a volunteer from each group to change the crown in their tree and use play dough to make a new one. Then have the group put oranges and count how many they were able to put on the crown.

In order for the crown to hold more oranges they need something harder, such as the play dough.

ABOVE LEVEL

Divide students into pairs. Ask, *How can you improve your tree to hold more oranges?* Have them analyze their own work and compare with their classmate's to see if it is the same or different. Ask, *Which material makes a strong crown?* Help students identify that the play dough is harder and can hold more oranges. Have them put oranges and count how many they were able to put on the crown.

CLOSING

Do a gallery walk. Say goodbye.

Materials and preparation
- Students' craft trees

Have students place their trees on their table. Do a gallery walk with students. Show them the path they will follow and allow them to comment on the different materials and number of oranges in the trees. Remind them to walk safely and not to crowd their classmates.
When they have seen all the trees, say *goodbye* to students and have them say *goodbye* back to you.

MATCH THE PLASTIC FOOD CONTAINERS WITH THEIR LID.

STEAM • WHAT IS YOUR FAVORITE FOOD? • UNIT 7

Learning goals
- Learn to put food away in the refrigerator and why this is necessary
- Use non-standard measuring tools to check which lid goes on each container
- Compare length and identify if it is the same or different

STEAM subjects
- Science
- Math

Thinking skills
Remembering, understanding, applying, analyzing, evaluating

Main language content
It's long. It's short.
The same. Different.
Food: *apple, banana, bread, cheese, cookie, lemon, pineapple, popsicle, tomato*
Cutlery: *lid, plastic container, plate*

OPENING

Circle time

Materials and preparation
- A bell
- Puppet
- Visual schedule pictures

Greet students and have them greet you back. Ask, *How are you?* and have students show their thumbs up to respond.
Have them sit in a circle. Place the visual schedule pictures face down in the circle. Have two students turn them over and say what activity they represent. Make the bell chime and say, *Can you hear the chime?*
Show a picture of one of today's activities and elicit, *It's (science) time!* Repeat with the other subject.

Math – Find the lids and place them correctly.

Materials and preparation
- A plate (plastic or glass)
- Two plastic food containers with lids

Hide the lids of the containers and have students remain in a circle. Show them the containers and the plate and ask, *What do we use this for? What do you put inside?* Allow students to brainstorm things they can put inside the containers. If they refer to items that are not edible, take their idea into consideration, too. Ask them to say where in their house they see these types of containers, in which one they eat, and finally ask which of them usually has a lid, a plate or a plastic container. Tell students there are two lids somewhere in the classroom and have them look for them. When they find the lids hold a container and ask, *Which lid goes on this container?* Have them guess first and invite a student to place the lid on top. Have another student close the other container.

ACTIVE LEARNING

Science – Putting food away in the refrigerator

Materials and preparation
- Flashcards: *cookies, popsicle*
- Two plastic containers with lids

Show students the two pictures and say, *I went to the supermarket. I bought cookies and popsicles.* Show students the flashcards as you say the words. Then say, *I don't want to eat now. I want to eat tomorrow.*

Draw a refrigerator on the board and teach students the word *refrigerator*. Ask, *Which one has to go in the refrigerator, the cookies, or the popsicles?* Have students give their answers and, before correcting them, say, *The refrigerator is cold. It's for cold food. Which one is cold?*

Ask students to talk about other food they see in the refrigerator in their houses and ask why they think the food goes in the refrigerator: *It needs to be cold. It can go bad when it is not cold.*

If possible, take the students to visit the school kitchen or cafeteria and see what is in the refrigerator.

Math – Match the plastic food containers with their lid.

Materials and preparation
- Crayons or pencils
- Markers
- Project Book page 59
- Wooden skewers (one per pair of students)

Help students open their Project Book to page 59. Say that these are food containers.

Have students check which lid goes on each container.

Divide them into pairs and give them the skewers. Have them place the skewer right above the lid and use a marker to draw a line as long as the lid. Then have them check which container top has that length. When they find it, have them match. Model first with one of the lids and containers on the page.

When checking answers, use a skewer to measure the lids and containers yourself while students help.

> **Note to teachers**
> Although the size of the lids and containers are visibly different, measuring provides students with a way of checking their choices and learning from making mistakes.

DIFFERENTIATED INSTRUCTION

BELOW LEVEL
Math – Find and measure.

Materials and preparation
- Wooden skewers cut into different sizes

Group students into pairs. Give each pair a skewer and have them look for something in the classroom that is as long as their skewer. Allow them to show their classmates from other pairs what they could find and have other pairs check their classmates' choices.

ABOVE LEVEL
Math – Compare, find, and measure.

Materials and preparation
- Wooden skewers cut into different sizes

Divide students into pairs. Give each pair two skewers of different lengths and ask them to say which one is longer. Then have them look for things in the classroom that are as long as both their skewers. Allow them to show their classmates from other pairs what they could find and have other pairs check their classmates' choices.

CLOSING

Make a line to say goodbye.

Materials and preparation
- Puppet

Have students line up according to how tall they are, from the shortest to the tallest. Help them organize themselves first. When they are lined up, have each one of them say *goodbye* to the puppet and to you and say what they liked most in today's class.

> **Note to teachers**
> Whenever possible, take pictures of your students while they are working to show them and have them think about their performance.

Unit 8 What do you like about school?

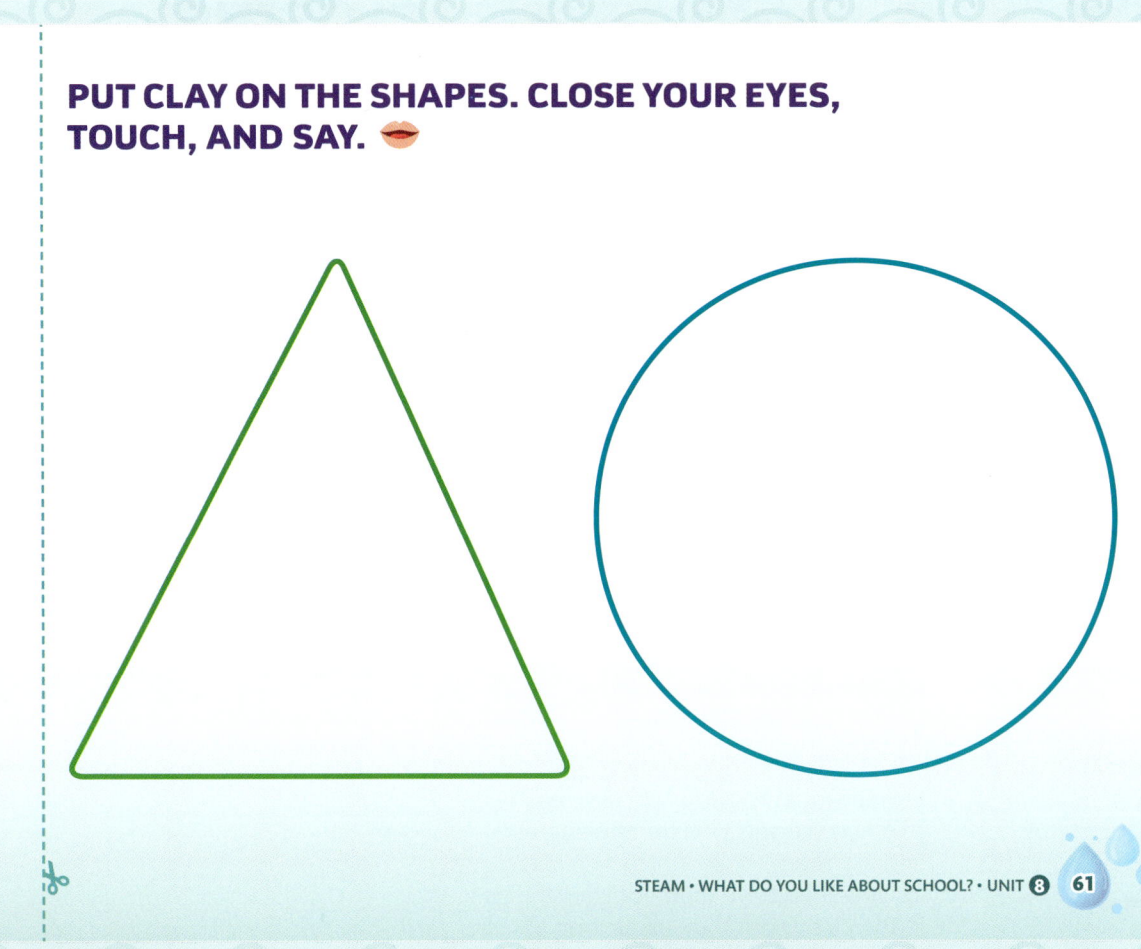

Learning goals
- Develop the sense of touch
- Learn about patterns and finding similarities in them
- Use pieces of triangles of different colors to make tessellation

STEAM subjects
- Science
- Arts
- Math

Thinking skills
Remembering, conceptualizing, applying, analyzing, creating, evaluate

Main language content
It's different. It's similar.
I have blue. My classmate has green.
Colors: *blue, green, orange, pink, purple, red, yellow*
Numbers: *1-10*
Shapes: *circle, square, triangle*

OPENING

Circle time

Materials and preparation
- A bell
- Puppet
- Visual schedule pictures

Say *hello* to students. Encourage them to say *hello* to you and the puppet. Make it answer, *Hello, my friends*.
Then place the visual schedule pictures face down in the circle. Call on a student to turn over a picture and show it to the rest of the class. Elicit the name of the subject. Make the bell chime and ask, *Can you hear the chime?* Elicit, *It's (arts) time!* Repeat with the other subjects.

Science – What's in the box of surprises?

Materials and preparation
- Box of surprises (a cardboard box with a hole to put the hand inside)
- Pattern blocks: *circle, square, triangle* (or objects that have these shapes)

The purpose of this activity is to guess the shape by only manipulating an item, without being able to see it.
Bring out the *box of surprises*. Put several plastic or wooden shapes in the box and tell students they will take turns putting their hands inside it. Have students call out the shape and take out the object to check if their guess was correct.

Note to teachers
Stimulating children's awareness of the five senses from a very young age helps them develop an intuitive knowledge of how their senses work before being formally introduced to them later on in school.

ACTIVE LEARNING

Science and arts – Put clay on the shapes. Close your eyes, touch, and say.

Materials and preparation
- Clay
- Project Book page 61

Help students open their Project Book to page 61. Show them the two shapes on the page and elicit the names. Give them clay and say that they need to put small pieces of clay to cover the inside of the shape and they can't go outside the outlines. Help students as needed. Have students work in pairs. One student closes their eyes and the other leads their classmate's hand to a clay shape on the page. They need to guess what shape it is just by touching it. Remind them to take turns.

Arts and math – Tiling art

Materials and preparation
- A picture of a honeycomb
- Glue
- Sheets of paper (one per student)
- Triangles (4x4x4cm) cut out from colored cardboard paper

Explain to students that tessellation or tiling is patterns made of shapes that fit together leaving no blank space between them. Demonstrate by placing six triangles together and forming a long rectangle: every other triangle must be upside down. Say that, in nature, they can see tessellation in honeycombs made by bees. Show them the picture as you say so. Give each student an empty sheet of paper and pieces of triangles to create their own pattern. Have them choose two of the colors available. Remind them that there can be no space between the triangles and remind them of your model. Help them glue the pieces on the paper and invite them to display their art when they have finished.

While they are working, help them count the triangles in their work.

Note to teachers
The art of tessellation dates back to the ancient Sumerians who used tiny geometric shapes to make mosaics from clay, stone, and glass tiles.

DIFFERENTIATED INSTRUCTION

BELOW LEVEL
Math – Compare and say if it is the same.

Materials and preparation
- Students' tiling artwork

Divide students into small groups and have them look for similarities in their patterns: the number of triangles they used and the colors. Walk around and encourage them to say what similarities they found: *I have blue triangles, too. My classmate has ten triangles and I have ten triangles, too.*

ABOVE LEVEL
Math – Compare similarities and differences.

Materials and preparation
- Students' tiling artwork

Divide students into small groups and have them look for similarities and differences in their patterns. Allow them to think about what in the patterns they can compare and make sure the color and number of triangles is included. Walk around and encourage them to say what similarities and differences they found: *I have blue and red triangles. My classmate has green and red triangles. My classmate has eight triangles and I have eight triangles, too.*

CLOSING

Make an art exhibit. Say goodbye.

Materials and preparation
- Students' tiling artwork

Choose an area in the school and have students place their artwork there. Tell them that they are going to be the artists presenting their work. If possible, invite other groups to visit their work; if not, have a few of them at a time visit their classmates' work. Encourage them to talk about their work, *They're triangles. They're blue and red triangles.*

After a while, take students back to the classroom and say *goodbye* to them.

DRAW THE SEQUENCE FOR THE MINDFULNESS ACTIVITY.

STEAM • WHAT DO YOU LIKE ABOUT SCHOOL? • UNIT 8

Learning goals
- Use mindfulness to relax and learn about their body reactions
- Think of a logical sequence of events

STEAM subjects
- Science
- Engineering
- Arts
- Math

Thinking skills
Understanding, applying, analyzing, creating

Main language content
Close your eyes. Open your eyes.
Touch your belly.
Breathe in. Breathe out.
School materials: book, crayon, marker, pen, pencil, pencil case

OPENING

Circle time

Materials and preparation
- A bell
- A book
- Puppet
- Visual schedule pictures

Say *hello* to students. Encourage them to say *hello* to you and the puppet. Make it answer, *Hello, my friends.*
Cover the pictures of today's schedule using a book. Hold the pictures behind the book and show part of them only. Ask students if they can guess what activity it is. Repeat with the other picture. Show one picture at a time, make the bell chime, and ask, *Can you hear the chime?*
Elicit, *It's (arts) time!* Repeat with the other subjects.

Science – Mindfulness

Materials and preparation
- Audio library – songs

Ask students to bring their chairs to the circle. Play a calm song and tell students to settle down and listen to you. Give them the following instructions and model:
1. Sit and close your eyes.
2. Put your hands on your belly.
3. Take a deep breath in: *one, two, three.*
4. Take a deep breath out: *one, two, three.*
Invite students to open their eyes and say what they could hear and if they liked being with their eyes closed and hands on their belly. They might talk about the song or any other noise they heard. They might even refer to sounds in their head that may be part of their imagination or thoughts. You can also ask them if they could hear their breath. Take a long *breath* in and out to show them what *breath* means. Let them speak freely.

Note to teachers
Mindfulness in education is a tool that helps students deal with moments of anxiety, stress, and anger. This way they learn about the reactions their body has.

ACTIVE LEARNING

Science and math – Draw the sequence for the mindfulness activity.

Materials and preparation
- Crayons or pencils
- Project Book page 63

Help students open their Project Book to page 63 and look at the pictures. Say that the students in the pictures are doing mindfulness activities that help them notice better what is around them now, like the activity they did before.
Tell students that the pictures are not in the correct order. Invite them to draw a line starting at the first picture and leading to the second. Remind them of what they did first: sit down and close your eyes. Have them identify the picture and start a line coming from it. Then ask if they remember what they did next and have them draw the line from the first picture to the one showing the children with their hands on their belly. Go on until they have reached the fourth picture.

Engineering – Think before building.

Materials and preparation
- A variety of school materials, such as crayons, glue stick, pencils, and pencil case
- Any decorative craft material you might have available
- Brushes
- Colored glue (optional)
- Colored paper
- Glue
- Markers
- Paint
- Shoe boxes (one per group)

Tell students that doing mindfulness exercises makes them feel relaxed, calm. Ask them in a low, relaxed voice, *Are you calm? Are you relaxed?* Tell them that now they are ready for a more challenging activity.
Put some of your school materials, such as pencil case, pencils, crayons, and glue stick on the table and say, *I have no where to put my materials! Can you help me?* Students might come up with suggestions to put things separately somewhere in the classroom. Explain that you want everything to be together in a place and you would like them to build something that can hold your things.
Divide them into groups and give them the materials. Give them some time to think of what to do.
Some ideas are to leave the shoe box with or without the lid, decorate it by gluing paper around it, painting it, using colored glue, using markers, drawing the materials that are inside using markers, etc.

DIFFERENTIATED INSTRUCTION

BELOW LEVEL
Engineering and arts – Make a case for the school materials.

Materials and preparation
- Materials listed in the previous activity

After students have thought of the possibilities for a while, have groups share their ideas with the whole class and give them suggestion of how they can improve their ideas. This way you will help them start thinking of possibilities to make their work better.

ABOVE LEVEL

Before sharing their thoughts, let students try to apply their ideas using the materials provided. Let them decorate their box however they like and see if it is effective in putting everything away.

Have groups exchange work and give each other suggestions on how to improve their work.

Note to teachers
Testing ideas and checking if they work help students learn the basics of hypothesizing and reflecting on process and result from an early age.

CLOSING

See if your idea works. Say goodbye.

Materials and preparation
- Materials for students to put in the case they made
- Students' craft case

Have students sit in a circle. Show them the materials they needed to help you put away again and have them test their work. Ask, *Can you put everything inside? Is the case good?*
Then thank them for their help, say *goodbye*, and elicit *goodbye*.

WHAT DOES YOUR SCHOOL LOOK LIKE? MAKE A POINTILLIST PAINTING.

STEAM • WHAT DO YOU LIKE ABOUT SCHOOL? • UNIT 8   65

Learning goals
- See how colors mix and form new colors
- Learn about a new painting technique
- Create an artwork of a school using pointillism

STEAM subjects
- Science
- Arts

Thinking skills
Remembering, understanding, applying, analyzing, creating

Main language content
What is it?
A school.
The roof is brown and orange.
Colors: *blue, brown, green, orange, purple, red, yellow*
Parts of a building: *door, roof, steps, wall, window*

OPENING

Circle time
Materials and preparation
- A bell
- Puppet
- Visual schedule pictures

Bring out the puppet and start by having it greet the students. After they greet the puppet, have the puppet greet you, too. Then elicit *hello* and ask students how they are today.

Hide the pictures representing today's schedule and have students look for them. Then place them in the circle. Make the bell chime and ask, *Can you hear the chime?* Ask students if they remember how to reply and help as needed.

Show a picture of one of today's activities and elicit, *It's (science) time!* Repeat with the other subjects.

Science and arts – Mixing colors
Materials and preparation
- Blue, red, and yellow paint
- Brushes
- Plastic containers or plates

Give each student a brush and an empty container. Explain to them that you are going to do some science today; you are going to mix colors to make new colors. Ask, *Have you tried this before? Do you know how to mix colors?*

Put a bit of yellow and a bit of blue in the containers and ask them to use their brushes to mix. Ask, *What color is it?* Elicit *green* from students. Do the same with yellow and red to make orange and blue and red to make purple. Elicit the names of the colors from students.

68 STEAM

ACTIVE LEARNING

Arts – Learning about pointillism

Materials and preparation
- Pictures of pointillist artwork
- Pictures of fruit, people, pets, toys etc.

Tell students that today they are going to learn about a new painting technique called *pointillism*. Make small dots on the board and as you do it, chant, *Point, point, point, point, pointillism!*
Explain that with this technique the painting is made entirely with small dots of one color.
Display the pictures of everyday items and ask students what they can see in each one. Ask, *Can you imagine these pictures made out of small dots?* Let them share with their classmates how they think it would look. Then show them some pointillist artwork and have them compare with the other pictures.

Arts – What does your school look like? Make a pointillist painting.

Materials and preparation
- Cotton swabs
- Paint
- Project Book page 65

Help students open their Project Book to page 65 and look at the picture. Ask, *What is it?* Elicit, *A school.* Have them look at the roof and ask, *What color is the roof?* Tell students that they are going to make their own school using pointillism. Give them a cotton swab and have them use brown paint to continue the roof.
Then have them choose colors for the rest of the school and continue to use the same technique.

DIFFERENTIATED INSTRUCTION

BELOW LEVEL
Play *Run and touch*.

Materials and preparation
- Masking tape
- Students' school pointillist artwork

Choose two of the pointillist paintings featuring different colors to place on the wall or on the floor using tape. Have students make a line facing the artwork and say an element of one of them, *The roof is brown and orange. The windows are blue.* Have the students, one at a time, run to the correct picture and tap the area next to it. Remind them not to touch the painting as it may still be a little wet.
After a while divide them into two groups and have students give the clues for their classmates to run and touch.

ABOVE LEVEL

Divide students into two groups. Choose three of the pointillist paintings per group featuring different colors to place on the wall or on the floor using tape. Have students in a group make a line facing their group's artwork and choose one student from each group to give clues on which picture to tap, *The roof is brown and orange. The windows are blue. The walls are green.* Have the students, one at a time, run to the correct picture and tap the area next to it. Remind them not to touch the painting as it may still be a little wet. Allow students to take turns being the one giving clues about the paintings.

CLOSING

Compare your masterpieces.

Materials and preparation
- Students' school pointillist artwork

Have students work in groups to show their school and compare their masterpiece with their classmates in terms of the colors they used in each part of it and how similar it is to their own school.

FIND THE BUGS. HOW CAN YOU FIX THEM?

STEAM • WHAT DO YOU LIKE ABOUT SCHOOL? • UNIT 8 • 67

Learning goals
- Get introduced to the term *debug*
- Learn to identify and fix mistakes and make something work well
- Make a playground slide and test it with a ball

STEAM subjects
- Technology
- Engineering
- Arts

Thinking skills
Remembering, understanding, applying, analyzing, creating

Main language content
It's a playground. It's a slide.
What's the problem here?
Let's debug this slide. Fix the slide.
Playground equipment: *slide, swing*

OPENING

Circle time

Materials and preparation
- A bell
- A book
- Puppet
- Visual schedule pictures

Say *hello* to students. Encourage them to say *hello* to you and the puppet. Make the puppet answer, *Hey, my friends! How are you?* Encourage them to answer.
Cover the pictures of today's schedule using a book. Hold the pictures behind the book and show part of them only. Ask students if they can guess what activity it is. Repeat with the other picture.
Show one picture at a time, make the bell chime, and ask, *Can you hear the chime?*
Elicit, *It's (technology) time!* Repeat with the other subject.

School tour

Walk around the classroom with your students and elicit what kind of activities you do in each part. Point to classroom items and elicit their names. Have students suggest activities they would like to do in each part.
Then take students for a school tour and have them talk about what they do in each part of the school. If possible, take them to the playground and show them a slide. Have them make the slide movement with their hand.

70 STEAM

ACTIVE LEARNING

Technology – Find the bugs. How can you fix them?

Materials and preparation
- Brushes
- Colored cutouts from magazines (as big as the bugs on the page)
- Glue
- Paint
- Project Book page 67

Help students open their Project Book to page 67. Show them the playground and ask what part of the school that is. Teach them the name of the equipment, *a slide, swings*. Tell students that you know the playground in the picture, and that a few hours later, two students got hurt in the playground. Say, *There are big problems in this playground, two bugs! Where are the bugs?* Let students analyze the picture for a while and comment on their findings. If necessary, point to the bug and have them identify why it is a problem.

Explain that they need to fix the bugs-debug the game for the children to play. Show them the materials and ask, *How can you fix this slide?* Let them think of ways to make a barrier where it is broken. When they are done, ask, *How can you fix the rope holding the swing?* and repeat the procedures.

Have students share their solutions with the class.

Engineering and arts – Make a slide. How can you improve it?

Materials and preparation
- Clay
- Markers
- Paper towel cardboard rolls (one per pair of students)

Divide students into pairs and give them some clay and a paper towel cardboard roll. Explain that they are going to make a slide for the school playground. Ask, *How can you go up the slide?* Remind students that there is a ladder to go up the slide and have them identify which item is their ladder (the cardboard roll). Have them draw the steps on one side.

Then tell students to use clay to make the slide. Allow them to think of how to do it for a while with their classmates. Let them test it in different ways and exchange ideas with each other.

When they finish, ask them to think of a way to make the slide better and safer. Pretend to be sliding down it and falling off the side. Help them identify that there should be barriers on the side of the slide and use clay to make them.

Note to teachers
Giving students materials to create something and letting them figure out by themselves or with just a little help how to build something are great ways to develop both logical and critical thinking as well as encourage students to become autonomous learners.

DIFFERENTIATED INSTRUCTION

BELOW LEVEL
Technology – Debug it!

Materials and preparation
- Popsicle sticks
- Small Styrofoam balls
- Students' slides

Divide students into small groups and have them get one of the slides. Break the popsicle stick so as to fit on the students' slide and connect both sides. Place it in the middle of the slide so as to create a barrier that prevents the ball from rolling down. Give students a Styrofoam ball and tell them to try to roll it down. They will notice that the ball either stops or rolls off of the slide because of the stick. Say, *Oops! There is a bug in your slide system. How can you fix it?* Help students identify that the popsicle stick is the "bug" and it needs to be removed to fix the problem. Have them test it and comment on the results.

ABOVE LEVEL

Divide students into pairs and do the procedures explained in *Below level* When the popsicle sticks are on the slides, have students try to roll the ball down. Roll a ball down a slide yourself, but choose one without a stick so that they can notice the difference. Don't tell them that there is a problem. Have them identify it alone. Once a pair of students has identified a problem, say, *What? Is there a bug? Where is it?* And have them identify the "bug", too. After removing the bug, have them test the slide again and comment on the results.

Note to teachers
Although students are introduced to the term *debug* in this lesson to refer to fixing a failure in a system, they might still take a while to connect it to failure and mistakes in processes, so repeating the term at the correct moments helps them start to understand what it means before moving to real computational systems.

CLOSING

Talk about your favorite part of the class and say goodbye.

Materials and preparation
- Puppet

Have students sit in a circle to revisit their activities today. After reviewing what they have done, ask, *Which one is your favorite?* and allow students to comment on the activities they had. Take their opinion into consideration when planning your next lessons or program.

Say *goodbye* to them and have them say *goodbye* to you, the puppet, and to each other.

Notes

Notes

Notes

Notes

Notes

Notes

Notes

Notes

Notes